WHAT CUSTOMERS WANT

WHAT CUSTOMERS WANT

USING OUTCOME-DRIVEN INNOVATION
TO CREATE BREAKTHROUGH
PRODUCTS AND SERVICES

ANTHONY ULWICK

McGraw·Hill

New York   Chicago   San Francisco   Lisbon   London   Madrid   Mexico City
Milan   New Delhi   San Juan   Seoul   Singapore   Sydney   Toronto

The **McGraw·Hill** Companies

Library of Congress Cataloging-in-Publication Data

Ulwick, Anthony W., 1957–
    What customers want : using outcome-driven innovation to create breakthrough products and services / by Anthony Ulwick.
       p.   cm.
    Includes index.
    ISBN 0-07-140867-3 (alk. paper)
    1. New products—Planning.   2. Product management.   1. Strategic planning.
I. Title.

    HF5415.153.U49   2005
    658.5′75—dc22   2005016744

15 16 17 18 19 20   DOC/DOC   1 9 8 7 6

ISBN 0-07-140867-3

McGraw-Hill books are available at special quantity discounts to use as premiums and sales promotions, or for use in corporate training programs. For more information, please write to the Director of Special Sales, Professional Publishing, McGraw-Hill, Two Penn Plaza, New York, NY 10121-2298. Or contact your local bookstore.

This book is printed on acid-free paper.

Dedicated to my parents, Lorena and Anthony W. Ulwick Sr.,
my sources of strength and discipline.

Contents

Acknowledgments

For almost two decades now I have been interested in understanding the process of innovation—the set of steps that people and companies take to create products and services that customers value. I have always believed that the process of innovation could somehow be broken down into steps and controlled by companies in such a way that they could achieve a consistent and predictable result—much like companies have accomplished with other business processes. In my journey to understand this process and help companies achieve this goal, I have had the great pleasure and honor to work with some of the most brilliant minds in this field. In the academic world, Harvard Business School professor Clayton M. Christensen has asked me hard questions and motivated me to solidify my ideas about outcome-driven innovation. His thinking and willingness to share those thoughts are greatly appreciated. Likewise, Harvard Business School professor Clark Gilbert has been exceptional at providing personal guidance and insight. They are both leaders in this field.

In the business world I have been blessed to work with exceptional individuals who are also motivated to demystify the innovation process. Jeff Baker, Jeff Hansen, Joel Block, Dave Wascha, Bobby Bakshi, Steven Silverman, and other researchers at Microsoft have spent countless hours contributing to the evolution of our outcome-driven thinking. Others who have selflessly contributed their time and thinking include Moira McGuire and Joe Post of Protocol; Michael Lee of Medtronic; Mike Favet of Guidant; Ken Dobler and Rick Faleschini of Johnson & Johnson; Michael Fons of Ecolab; Kim Westover of J. R. Simplot; Paul Zarookian of Imperial A.I. Credit Corporation; Judy Maritato, Randall Coe, Andrew Reed, and Jason Schickerling of Robert Bosch Tool Corporation; David Lund of Chiquita; Dr. Jerome Grossman of the Harvard Kennedy School of Government; Linda Applestein of Rohm and Haas Company; Matthew Nightingale of MeadWestvaco; Marshall Kostiuk of Syngenta; Dave Hotchkiss of Coloplast; Kevin Reeth and Michael Maron of Intuit; Robert Leonhardt and Eric Eskey of HP; and Ben Allen of Kroll Ontrack.

Most importantly, I have a profound debt to all my colleagues here at Strategyn. The contributions made by Sandy Bates, Dr. Robert Pennisi, Dr. Lance Bettencourt, Rob Schade, Chris Cordes, Andrew Johnson, Bill Nordeen, Roger Chevalier, Jerry Rossow, Matt Graham, and Joseph Winiarski have been discerning and valuable. Their ongoing inputs and improvements to our innovation process have accelerated its evolution. They are a great team who compliment and motivate each other to excellence. I'd also like to give special thanks to Sandy Bates and Andrew Johnson for their efforts and support in editing and preparing this book for publication.

As peers, Matt Eyring, Mark Johnson, and Scott Anthony, who are all part of Clayton M. Christensen's team at Innosight, have provided me with not only friendship but constant support and a partnership that has been enjoyable and rewarding—I wish them ongoing success.

Lastly, I owe the deepest debt to my son, Anthony, and my wife, Heather, for sacrificing with me as we spent time apart so that this book could be written. I thank them for sharing my joy, being patient, and giving me encouragement as it was needed.

Over the past twenty years I have traveled many roads and enjoyed meeting dozens of wonderful, insightful, motivated, and brilliant people. They have taught me much about innovation. I thank all of you who have made this a joyful, rewarding, and meaningful experience for me and for the chance to share this knowledge.

Introduction

Moving Beyond the Customer-Driven Paradigm

In the mid-1980s business leaders began to recognize that being technology driven was just not good enough. Up until that point it was common for companies to create a new technology and then attempt to find markets in which the technology could flourish. The traditional Research and Development (R&D) laboratories, such as Bell Labs, were in jeopardy because they struggled to produce many products that customers wanted. Motorola's Iridium project, which sought to build a mass-market business for a product that appealed to only a narrow demographic, for example, cost Motorola more than $5 billion to build and ultimately sold for $25 million—about half a penny for every dollar it originally cost. The system, which required users to buy phones that cost about $3,000 each and placed calls at $7 a minute, had little appeal. They gambled on a market that was not there.[1]

As the process improvement craze swept corporate America, many companies realized just how costly it was to continue to use this trial-and-error approach to innovation. With failure rates approaching 90 percent, R&D expenditures under scrutiny, and lead times for success averaging nearly eight years, it was clear that a new approach was needed.

---

1. Arik Hesseldahl, "The Return of Iridium," Forbes.com (November 30, 2001).

Out of necessity, companies began to adopt the ideas and principles associated with the customer-driven movement. Its basic tenet is that companies should understand what their customers want before they invest in the creation of a new product or service. This commonsense approach was aimed squarely at making the innovation process more efficient. Using the customer-driven approach, companies began to conduct customer interviews and act on the feedback they received. They performed ethnographic and anthropological research. They began to test product concepts with users. Indeed, over the past two decades qualitative and quantitative research methods have become corporate staples. Focus groups, customer visits, conjoint analysis, needs-based segmentation, and lead-user analysis have become tools of the trade. Customer-driven thinking is well entrenched and has become the mantra of the corporate world. But after twenty years of customer-driven thinking, U.S. companies still find that 50 to 90 percent of their product and service initiatives are failures, collectively costing them more than $100 billion each year. Consider how New Coke, a customer-driven product initiative that involved one of the most exhaustive market-research projects in history with almost 200,000 consumer interviews at a cost of $4 million, resulted in one of the most embarrassing product failures of all time.[2] Of the initiatives that do succeed, only a few are truly innovative. The conclusion? Although some improvements have been made, being customer driven is just not good enough. There is still too much variance.

With the growing importance of innovation in today's globalizing economy and an unprecedented need for market growth, it is clear that a new approach is needed. Companies must take innovation to the next level—but how? The answer is rooted in the funda-

---

2. Robert M. Schindler, "The Real Lesson of New Coke: The Value of Focus Groups for Predicting the Effects of Social Influence," *Marketing Research* (December 1992), 25.

mentals of business process improvement. Thirty-five years ago when production managers were experiencing manufacturing yields as low as 10 percent, they turned to Six Sigma principles and tools such as statistical process control (SPC) to improve the quality levels and predictability of the manufacturing process. The same thinking can be applied to the innovation process: by identifying the stages of innovation and eliminating the factors that introduce variability into the innovation process, companies can realize higher innovation success rates and more breakthrough products and services.

I first began to think about innovation as a process in 1984, the day after my colleagues and I at IBM (my employer at the time) introduced the PCjr. The *Wall Street Journal* immediately declared the machine a flop—in big, bold type. It had taken the press just a day to deem the product into which we had put our hearts, souls, and minds, not to mention a million dollars in market research for the past eighteen months, an unmitigated failure. What did they know that we didn't? Why hadn't we let members of the press review the product earlier so we could have anticipated their reaction? What criteria had they used to judge the PCjr's value? If we had known their criteria in advance, could we have designed the product differently to ensure a more positive response?

One fact was undeniable: the PCjr was a flop, one that cost IBM well over half a billion dollars before it was pulled from the market in 1985. The traditional customer-driven tools we used to define and test the product let us down. At the time, I couldn't be sure exactly where the process had failed, but I couldn't let go of a recurring thought. It seemed to me that if we knew, well in advance, what criteria customers were going to use to judge a product's value, we could dutifully design a product that met those criteria—and that product would be a success. But wasn't that what the customer-driven approach was supposed to be all about—asking customers what they wanted and then delivering on their requests? If so, where had the process gone wrong? Why had it failed us?

In years of analyzing the customer-driven approach to innovation, I have discovered one factor that stands out above all others in derailing the customer-driven approach and in introducing process variability. Ironically, it is the inputs that come from the customer—that's right, the customer's requirements. When companies gather customer requirements they do not know what types of inputs they need to obtain from the customer. Neither does the customer. Consequently, the customer offers his requirements in a language that is convenient to him, but unfortunately that language is not particularly convenient for the creation of breakthrough products. Paradoxically, the literal voice of the customer does not translate into meaningful inputs. In fact, the customer-driven movement has failed to produce the desired results because asking the customer what he wants solicits not only the wrong inputs, but inputs that inadvertently cause the failures that managers are fervently trying to avoid. Companies have attempted to identify opportunities, segment markets, conduct competitive analysis, and brainstorm new product and service ideas based on these faulty inputs.

To figure out what customers want and to successfully innovate, companies must think about customer requirements very differently. Companies must be able to know, well in advance, what criteria customers are going to use to judge a product's value and dutifully design a product that ensures those criteria are met. These criteria must be predictive of success and not lagging indicators.

I have spent the years since the PCjr fiasco defining just what inputs companies must capture from customers in order to innovate successfully. The quest begins with language. An agreed-on language is fundamental to success in any discipline, yet confusion has permeated product development because companies continue to define "requirements" as any kind of customer input: customer wants, needs, benefits, solutions, ideas, desires, demands, specifications, and so on. But really, those are all different types of inputs, none of which can be used predictably to ensure success.

Along the way, I've created a more effective approach to innovation: I call it the outcome-driven method. It is a new way to think about the innovation process. Three key tenets define this approach.

- *Customers buy products and services to help them get jobs done.* In our study of new and existing markets we find that customers (both people and companies) have "jobs" with functional dimensions to them that arise regularly and need to get done. When customers become aware of such a job, they look around for a product or service that will help them get the job done. We know, for example, that people buy mowers so they can cut their lawns; they buy insurance to limit their financial risks; and they buy MP3 devices so they can manage and enjoy their music. Likewise, businesses buy servers to manage their e-mail; they hire consulting firms to formulate strategies; and they license Customer Relationship Management (CRM) seats to manage lead generation. Corn farmers, to take another example, buy corn seed, herbicides, pesticides, and fertilizers to help them grow corn. Carpenters buy circular saws to cut wood. Virtually all products and services are acquired to help get a job done. In the outcome-driven paradigm the focus is not on the customer, it is on the job: the job is the unit of analysis. When companies focus on helping the customer get a job done faster, more conveniently, and less expensively than before, they are more likely to create products and services that the customer wants. Only after a company chooses to focus on the job, not the customer, are they capable of reliably creating customer value.
- *Customers use a set of metrics (performance measures) to judge how well a job is getting done and how a product performs.* Just as companies use metrics to measure the output quality of a business process, customers use metrics to measure success in getting a job done. Customers have these metrics in their minds, but they seldom articulate them, and companies rarely understand them. We call these metrics the customers' desired outcomes. They are the fundamen-

tal measures of performance inherent to the execution of a specific job. When corn farmers grow corn, for example, they may judge products for their ability to minimize the number of seeds that fail to germinate, increase the percentage of plants that emerge at the same time, or minimize the yield loss owing to excess heat during pollination. When cutting wood with a circular saw, carpenters may judge products for their ability to minimize the likelihood of losing sight of the cut line, the time it takes to adjust the depth of the blade, or the frequency of kickbacks. For any given job, customers collectively apply 50 to 150 metrics (not just a handful) to measure how well the job is getting done. Only when all the metrics for a given job are well satisfied are customers able to execute the job perfectly. Ironically, these metrics are overlooked in the customer-driven world because they are not revealed by listening to the "voice of the customer."

  • *These customer metrics make possible the systematic and predictable creation of breakthrough products and services.* With the proper inputs in hand, companies dramatically improve their ability to execute all other downstream activities in the innovation process, including their ability to identify opportunities for growth, segment markets, conduct competitive analysis, generate and evaluate ideas, communicate value to customers, and measure customer satisfaction. In the outcome-driven paradigm, for example, companies do not brainstorm hundreds of ideas and then struggle to figure out which, if any, have value. Instead they figure out which of the 50 to 150 outcomes for a given job are important and unsatisfied and then systematically devise a few ideas that will better satisfy those underserved outcomes. Since they know which outcomes are *underserved*, they know where to make improvements, and, more importantly, they know doing so will result in products that customers want. If, for example, a drug-infusion-pump manufacturer knows that 90 percent of pain-management nurses are trying to minimize the time it takes to implement a dose change (but struggle to do so today), then they know not only where to focus their creativity, but also that time spent doing so will result in ideas that are worthy of pursuit. This flips the innovation process on its head.

So what are the implications of these tenets? Only after knowing what jobs customers are trying to get done and what outcomes they are trying to achieve are companies able to systematically and predictably identify opportunities and create products and services that deliver significant new value. Only then can they figure out *What Customers Want.*

Having the right inputs is critical to success, but knowing how to apply them is, too. The methods for doing so are described in this book. Once the outcomes for a given job are identified, for example, they must be prioritized and targeted. When a company knows which outcomes are most underserved and has chosen them as growth targets, then the company is able to:

- Optimize their messaging strategy and exploit the advantages their current products have in satisfying the targeted under-served outcomes
- Prioritize projects in their development pipeline so they can quickly bring to market those products and services that do the best job of addressing other targeted opportunities
- Systematically devise ideas that address the remaining unexploited opportunities, creating valuable if not breakthrough products

For example, when in 1994 the medical-device company Cordis Corporation targeted fifteen underserved outcomes in an attempt to grow share in the angioplasty balloon market, they realized that their current products already addressed three of those outcomes—they just never told anybody. To exploit these product advantages they refined their messaging and sales strategy and touted how their products addressed these newly-discovered opportunities. Their market share went from 1 to 5 percent within six months based purely on new messaging. Next, they looked at the development pipeline and recognized that the *stent*, a slender rod that supports blood vessels—which was one of about forty projects in the development pipeline—specifically addressed an extremely important but unsatisfied outcome, minimizing restenosis, which is the recurrence of the blockage. In response, they reprioritized their development resources, placing more developers on the stent, so they could get it out quickly and in doing so succeeded in becoming the first to bring such a product to market. The stent turned out to be the fastest growing medical device in history, one that created a billion dollar business for Cordis in less than two years. But they did not stop there. Lastly, they devised a new set of product features that addressed the remaining dozen or so underserved outcomes and one and a half years later released a line of angioplasty balloon products that took them from 5 to 20 percent market share, making them the angioplasty balloon market leader as well.

Factors That Introduce Variability into the Innovation Process

Before we get into the details of the outcome-driven approach to innovation, managers must first be willing to accept that innovation is indeed a science—a systematic process for creating products or services that delivers new value to customers—and not an art form that is forever destined to produce random and unpredictable results. Technically speaking, innovation is the process of creating a product or service solution that delivers significant new customer value. The process begins with the selection of the customer and market, includes the identification and prioritization of opportunities, and ends with the creation of an innovative product concept that delivers the new and significant value.

In more practical terms, innovation is simply the process of figuring out "what customers want." But, as I'll explain throughout this book, companies need to parse this phrase on two levels: companies must figure out not only what solutions and product features customers want, but as a prerequisite to devising a valued solution a company must first be able to figure out just what outcomes customers want the product to satisfy. In other words, companies need to figure out what jobs customers want to get done and how they measure success in getting a job done before they can determine what solutions customers want.

Although failure to obtain the right customer inputs is one major factor contributing to innovation failures, it is not the only factor that introduces variability into the innovation process. The wrong inputs make it difficult to obtain good results, but understanding the customer's desired outcomes by no means guarantees success. Companies must know for whom they want to create value and how to process and apply these inputs to create that value.

My colleagues and I have spent about twenty years defining the stages of the innovation process and identifying the factors that create variability in innovation results. We've analyzed the innovation processes and operations at dozens of companies in a myriad of industries and countries, looking for the factors that have made breakthrough innovations at these organizations random rather than predictable. We've identified eight such factors that introduce variability into the innovation process, each of which can be associated with an important stage in that process. Because they destabilize the innovation process, these factors are the root cause of many failed initiatives. Specifically, we've found that companies struggle with:

- Ill-conceived growth strategies
- Faulty data collection
- Missed opportunities
- Poor market segmentation
- Wrong growth targets
- Unfocused marketing, messaging, and branding
- Poorly prioritized development initiatives
- Scattershot idea generation

When you consider these eight factors, it's not surprising that the innovation process continues to appear random and unpredictable. But it is surprising that these inefficiencies have been tolerated for so long. In the past two decades, managers have integrated more metrics into their operations, and calculated returns are expected for every business endeavor. Nothing is left to speculation, ambivalence, or chance—except when it comes to a company's innovation process, which because of its creative nature has somehow managed to elude scrutiny.

Managers have come to expect that more than half their innovation initiatives will fail. To compensate, companies commonly invest in dozens of initiatives and hope that those that succeed will recoup the investments made in those that fail. This undisciplined approach is not only wasteful, it also directs resources away from opportunities that are truly worthy of pursuit, resulting in the loss of countless billions in opportunity costs. Imagine if companies only developed solutions they knew in advance would successfully address underserved customer outcomes. Imagine if all the resources being wasted on initiatives that will ultimately fail were placed on fewer initiatives that were likely to succeed. This is not fantasy; achieving these goals is possible today. But to realize this dream, companies need to adopt a new approach—one that defies conventional thinking.

Eight Steps to Outcome-Driven Innovation

What Customers Want introduces the idea of "outcome-driven" innovation. These concepts are relevant to companies that are ready to move beyond the customer-driven paradigm. This book was designed to help companies that want to achieve growth in their core markets, businesses that want to enter new markets, and firms that are looking to discover brand-new markets. In each of these scenarios the factors that can derail innovation efforts are usually

Figure FM.1   The Outcome-Driven Innovation Process

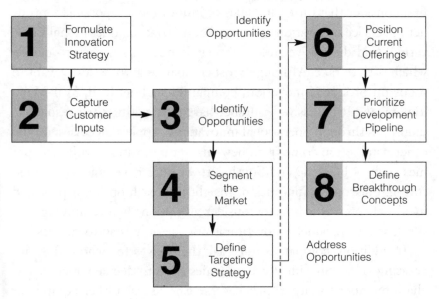

present in some form or another. These can be overcome, however, by using a standard eight-step approach that is outlined in the ensuing chapters. One step is covered in each chapter. It is important to remember that these steps define the outcome-driven innovation process. The process is shown in Figure FM.1.

Chapter 1, "Formulating the Innovation Strategy: Who Is the Target of Value Creation and How Should It Be Achieved?" sets the stage for a successful innovation initiative as it addresses questions such as:

- What types of innovation are possible?
- What growth options should be considered?
- Where in the value chain should we focus to maximize value creation?
- How do we handle multiple constituents with potentially conflicting outcomes?

Before embarking on any innovation initiative, companies must first consider that different types of innovation are possible—product or service innovation, new-market innovation, operational innovation, and disruptive innovation. It is not always easy to decide which path to take. Although most companies automatically want to focus on product innovation, companies such as Dell, Wal-Mart, Toyota, and Progressive Insurance have risen within their respective industries through operational innovations. Apple's successes, on the other hand, often come from new-market innovation, while companies such as E*Trade and Southwest Airlines have enjoyed success through disruptive innovation. Insight into each option is provided in this chapter. It is best to consider all options before moving forward, as new product innovation is not the only road to success.

In addition, companies must ask themselves for whom they are creating value. Specifically, companies need to decide which value-chain member to target: purchasers? End users? Other equipment manufacturers? Multiple customers in the chain? For some companies, making this decision can be a challenge. For instance, those companies far back in the value chain (such as producers of raw materials or makers of semiconductors) often talk with only OEMs and fail to directly consider the outcomes of other parties in the chain, such as purchasers or end users. Meanwhile, companies that have strong channel partners (such as makers of appliances and power tools) may not talk to end users directly and instead accept the channel partners' lists of end-user requirements as gospel, falsely assuming they have a good handle on what customers want. And still other companies (such as device manufacturers) often fail to consider an important customer in the value chain (IT directors, for instance) and only focus on end users. To formulate an effective innovation strategy, companies must correctly determine who in the value chain makes the most important judgments about value and go to them directly to understand what metrics they use to make those judgments. Once a company has figured out which customers to target and what type of innovation to pursue, the data collection process can begin.

Chapter 2, "Capturing Customer Inputs: Silence the 'Voice of the Customer'—Let's Talk Jobs, Outcomes, and Constraints," defines the types of inputs that are captured using traditional customer-driven methods (solutions, specs, needs, and benefits) and the types of inputs that must be captured in order to transform innovation into a predictable process—jobs and outcomes.

Getting these inputs right simplifies many other downstream activities associated with innovation, which means that identifying these jobs and outcomes is one of the most critical business processes in any organization. As we demonstrate through this book, with the proper inputs in hand, development and marketing managers dramatically enhance their ability to identify opportunities for growth, segment markets, conduct competitive analyses, generate and evaluate ideas, generate intellectual property, communicate value to customers, and measure customer satisfaction. They are dependent on obtaining these inputs to ensure their success. What is surprising then is the lack of precision that currently exists in defining what types of inputs are needed.

Listening to the "voice of the customer" has been the marketing mantra for more than twenty years, but it is time for that voice to be silenced. The literal voice of the customer sidetracks the innovation process because customers are not qualified to know what solutions are best—that is the job of the organization. And other inputs offered by customers (for example, statements such as "faster," "easy-to-use," "reliable," "smart," "powerful," "durable," "cheaper," and "better"), are far too vague to have any meaningful value to designers and engineers. By standardizing the collection and processing of the needed inputs within a structured framework, companies can transform innovation from an unstructured and random customer-driven process into a rules-based discipline. Chapter 2 focuses on the following questions:

- Why should companies gather customer requirements?
- What three issues plague the requirements-gathering process?
- What types of data do companies commonly collect from customers?
- What customer inputs are needed to master the innovation process?
- What methods should companies use to obtain the necessary information?
- How do you know which of the three types of inputs you should capture?

Chapter 3, "Identifying Opportunities: Discovering Where the Market Is Underserved and Overserved," describes how the customer's inputs are prioritized so as to reveal the big opportunities for growth and innovation. Outcomes that are important and unsatisfied are said to be *underserved* and represent opportunities for improvement, while those that are unimportant and well satisfied are said to be *overserved* and represent opportunities for cost reduction. These insights are critical to success in new-product, new-market, operational, and disruptive innovation. Only when all the desired outcomes of all the customers are known can the best opportunities be identified and prioritized.

Simply stated, innovation is a two-step process in which companies must identify opportunities *and* address them with new ideas. Companies rarely have trouble coming up with new ideas; what they lack is not creativity but direction. Without direction, however, developers are more likely to formulate product or service concepts that improve performance along dimensions that are already satisfied—adding no perceived value. They are also more likely to develop new features that add value in one area but negatively impact performance along other, more important, dimensions. Guessing where the opportunities are (and guessing wrong) introduces variability into the innovation process, making it difficult for companies to consistently devise breakthrough concepts.

Knowing what outcomes are important and unsatisfied is not the only challenge. Even companies that have good inputs seldom prioritize them well, and therefore they fail to allocate their resources optimally. The quantitative methods we have developed to accurately identify and prioritize opportunities are described in detail in this chapter. In discussing opportunity, Chapter 3 addresses the following questions:

- What is an opportunity?
- What three common mistakes are made in prioritizing opportunities?
- How should companies prioritize opportunities?
- How do you identify underserved and overserved markets?
- How does value migrate over time?
- What implications does the outcome-driven paradigm have for competitive analysis?

Chapter 4, "Segmenting the Market: Using Outcome-Driven Segmentation to Discover Segments of Opportunity," presents new methods for market segmentation and market discovery. Most companies do not segment their markets in ways that are optimal for successful innovation. Ideally, they would segment their markets to uncover those groups of customers that have unique sets of underserved outcomes. But for decades, it has been common practice for companies to group their customers by such attributes as needs, role, product type, price point, age, risk aversion, or other demographic or psychographic classifications. This practice may be convenient for the company and effective for some marketing- or sales-tracking purposes, but it thwarts the process of innovation. The only way to find a group of customers with a set of underserved outcomes is to use that variable as a means for segmentation. Can customers in different age groups or businesses of different sizes share common sets of underserved outcomes? Of course they can. Companies that do uncover these segments of opportunity can find new sources of innovation, new markets for disruptive technologies, and even opportunities in mature markets. These concepts are referenced by Harvard Business School professor Clayton M. Christensen in his recent book, *The Innovator's Solution*. The following questions are addressed in Chapter 4:

- What is the purpose of segmentation?
- How has the practice of segmentation evolved?
- Why are traditional segmentation methods ineffective for purposes of innovation?
- What is different about outcome-based segmentation?
- How is outcome-based segmentation performed?
- How does outcome-based segmentation address development and marketing challenges?
- How is job-based segmentation different, and when should it be used?

Chapter 5, "Targeting Opportunities for Growth: Deciding Where to Focus the Value Creation Effort," describes how outcome-driven companies decide which underserved and overserved outcomes to select as targets for growth, innovation, and cost reduction. When the opportunities for improvement have been revealed in a market, company managers must decide which ones to pursue. An effective targeting strategy adds function and performance—but not necessarily cost—in areas that are underserved and reduces cost and function in areas that are overserved. Through effective targeting, a company is able to optimize its product and service offerings so they deliver all the performance that can be absorbed but no more, so that customers are not paying for function they do not need.

Companies that do not have this insight make a number of mistakes in deciding where to focus their resources. For example, they are more likely to focus on the opportunities they *can* address, rather than those they *should* address. The opportunities they can address (perhaps because they are less technical or more interesting to work on than other initiatives) may not be the ones that offer the best chance for success. Such companies also tend to focus on what they do best and keep improving products along the same dimensions, even when the underlying outcomes are already well satisfied. A polymers producer, for example, may continually redesign a compound to be stronger and stronger, boosting costs as it goes, without realizing that the compound is strong enough. The customer is overserved, the product costs more, and no real value is added. Lastly, these uninformed companies often hesitate to move outside their core competencies—mostly because they are uncertain that such a movement and investment will result in success. If they knew for sure which outcomes were underserved, they could defend a decision and muster the resources to develop new competencies that would address those opportunities. The following questions are answered in Chapter 5:

- What is different about targeting for innovation?
- What types of broad-market opportunities are likely to be attractive?
- What segment-specific targeting strategies are effective?
- How does a targeting strategy result in a unique and valued competitive position?
- Why do companies fail to target key opportunities?

Chapter 6, "Positioning Current Products: Connecting Opportunities with Valued Product Features," introduces outcome-driven methods for positioning existing products, new products, and company brands and for creating communications that solidly connect with target customers. Once again, knowledge of the customer's outcomes enhances a company's ability to position and message effectively.

Once a company has targeted the best opportunities for growth, they must see if any of their current products address the underserved outcomes represented by those opportunities. If they do, the company is in a great position to exploit those opportunities for purposes of revenue gain. A company often finds some of their products address one or more underserved outcomes but that the company has failed to properly communicate those products' value. The messaging strategy that is most effective is the one that clearly states a product's advantage in areas of the market that are highly underserved.

Companies also struggle over whether to base their messaging strategies on the functional jobs and outcomes their customers are trying to achieve or whether to focus their messaging on an emotional dimension. This chapter explains why companies should stay focused on functional messaging when their product is functionally complex and has low emotional appeal (for example, the medical device and financial services industries), and why companies should focus on both function and emotion when they are in an industry that makes products that define the customer's persona, for example, the clothing and automobile industries. Chapter 6 explores the following questions:

- Why does messaging often fail to tout a product's true value?
- What are the prerequisites for an effective messaging strategy?
- What messaging will be most effective?
- Should a company message along an emotional or functional dimension?
- How does the sales force have immediate impact on revenue generation?
- What is the advantage of an outcome-based brand?

Chapter 7, "Prioritizing Projects in the Development Pipeline: Separating the Winners from the Losers," considers the products and services that companies have in development. Do any of them do a good job of satisfying customers' underserved outcomes? Those that do should be given high priority and receive the resources that are needed to get them to market quickly. Those products that don't should be aborted, as they will fail to deliver additional customer value.

Most companies don't know which product and service concepts will be winners and which will be failures. As a result, managers feel compelled to cover all the bases; they initiate hundreds of development efforts, spread resources too thin, and are reluctant to kill projects already under way—all of which creates inefficiencies in innovation. Chapter 7 offers methods for prioritizing products and services in the development pipeline and for evaluating new product and services ideas. Using this methodology, companies can determine which products successfully address underserved customer outcomes and which do not. Knowing which products in the pipeline are most likely to generate growth and revenue represents a true operational competitive advantage. Chapter 7 answers the following questions:

- What issues do companies face when prioritizing projects?
- What method is used to identify the winners and the losers?
- Which efforts should get top priority?
- What other factors affect project prioritization?

Chapter 8, "Devising Breakthrough Concepts: Using Focused Brainstorming and the Customer Scorecard to Create Customer Value," discusses the third option for growth—brainstorming new ideas. In a typical brainstorming session, employees do not know where the opportunities for improvement are, and consequently, their creativity is unfocused. Managers are forced to adopt a scattershot approach to idea generation, encouraging employees to generate ideas along many dimensions—product performance, pricing, distribution, marketing, and service. The success of a typical brainstorming session is often judged by the number of ideas generated rather than by the quality of the ideas generated—in part because there is no good way to evaluate the ideas. Introducing hundreds of irrelevant ideas into the innovation process, however, adds unneeded complexity and often bogs things down. In reality, companies do not need hundreds of new ideas; what they need is a handful of ideas that address important areas of opportunity. But they can only generate those useful ideas when they are focused on a set of targeted outcomes and apply focused brainstorming methods.

The concept creation process requires not only idea generation, but also idea evaluation. In the customer-driven environment, the methods used for concept evaluation are often flawed, bringing unwanted variability to the process. The outcome-based approach, by contrast, makes use of the customer scorecard, which lets companies evaluate ideas against customers' desired outcomes. This approach eliminates much of the error that is introduced by traditional evaluation methods and enables the systematic creation of new and potentially breakthrough concepts. Chapter 8 addresses the following questions:

- Why does traditional brainstorming often fail to produce breakthrough ideas?
- How are breakthrough concepts successfully generated?
- What are the mechanics behind focused brainstorming?
- Why do traditional concept-evaluation methods fail?
- How is the customer scorecard used to evaluate product and service concepts?
- How are these methods applied in practice?
- What is the role of R&D in the innovation process?

In this book, we explore many questions business leaders have wrestled with for decades in their quest to perfect the inherently flawed concepts associated with the customer-driven movement. The major differences between the traditional customer-driven approach to innovation and the outcome-driven approach defined herein are summarized in Table FM.1.

Over the past eighteen years, my colleagues and I have developed the thinking and methodology featured in this book, and for the past twelve years we have overseen its successful application in companies in nearly every industry. Our thinking has been adopted by

Table FM.1   Evolving the Process of Innovation

Stages of Innovation	Customer-Driven Approach	Outcome-Driven Approach	Benefits of the Outcome-Driven Approach
Formulate an innovation strategy	Companies focus on their core markets; other growth strategies are considered too risky.	Companies consider multiple avenues for product, market, operational, and disruptive innovation.	Companies devise attractive growth strategies that have high growth potential and a high probability for success.
Capture customer inputs	Companies listen to the "voice of the customer" and struggle to make sense out of vague inputs in order to give customers the solutions they request.	Companies determine what outcomes customers want to achieve and let qualified experts, not customers, devise the best solutions.	Marketing and development managers have the customer inputs they need to create solutions of significant value.
Identify areas of opportunity	Companies define "opportunities" as the solutions customers say they want. They prioritize innovation initiatives based on available resources and existing core competencies.	Companies define "opportunities" as the outcomes customers say are important and unsatisfied. They find the resources and build the competencies to address them.	Managers know where to focus employee creativity to create customer value. Companies don't waste time and effort on outcomes that are already overserved.
Segment the market	Customers are conveniently classified by product type, price point, age, risk aversion, and other demographic and psychographic characteristics.	Customers are segmented based on the outcomes they are trying to achieve. They are not placed into artificial, company-imposed classifications.	Managers are able to discover segments of opportunity in markets where few if any opportunities appear to exist, revealing new avenues for growth.

Table FM.I Evolving the Process of Innovation, *continued*

Stages of Innovation	Customer-Driven Approach	Outcome-Driven Approach	Benefits of the Outcome-Driven Approach
Target opportunities for growth	Companies pursue ideas that are intuitively attractive, easy to develop, or that fit within the firm's core competencies.	Companies pursue underserved and overserved outcomes for improvement and cost reduction, respectively.	Companies proactively define a competitive position that is unique and valued and then devise solutions to occupy that position.
Assess messaging and branding	Companies are uncertain if their positioning and messaging is tied to the customers' underserved outcomes.	Products and brands are tied directly to the emotional jobs or functional outcomes customers are trying to achieve.	Messaging connects solidly with customers and enhances the sales of existing and new products.
Prioritize projects in the development pipeline	Managers are compelled to cover all bases. They initiate hundreds of development efforts, spread resources too thin, and are reluctant to kill projects already under way.	Companies evaluate products in the pipeline for their ability to address the customers' underserved outcomes.	Companies know which initiatives will create the most value. They are able to create more winning products in less time and at less cost.
Devise breakthrough ideas	Employees brainstorm without focus, generating hundreds of ideas with questionable value. Many ideas must be evaluated.	Employees use focused brainstorming to direct their energies toward specific underserved outcomes and generate a few ideas of significant value.	Employees don't waste their time generating ideas that do not add value. They generate only ideas that are worthy of pursuit.

some of the world's most admired companies, including Microsoft, Johnson & Johnson, Bosch, AIG, and J. R. Simplot. We, along with many thought leaders and organizations, view it as the future of innovation. We encourage you to explore our ideas and to challenge our thinking so we can collectively help the innovation process evolve, enabling companies and countries worldwide to benefit from making innovation a more predictable discipline.

In addition to the chapters that discuss the eight-step approach to outcome-driven innovation, I have included an epilogue that offers executives and managers some practical tips on implementing the methodology, and a glossary of terms that provides companies with a common language for discussing and managing innovation.

WHAT
CUSTOMERS
WANT

CHAPTER

Formulating the Innovation Strategy

Who Is the Target of Value Creation and How Should It Be Achieved?

- *What types of innovation are possible?*
- *What growth options should be considered?*
- *Where in the value chain should we focus to maximize value creation?*
- *How do we handle multiple constituents with potentially conflicting outcomes?*

The first step in the innovation process is to define the innovation strategy. Specifically, companies need to figure out what type of innovation initiative they're going to pursue; what growth options are best; and who in the value chain should be targeted to maximize value creation in the market. They must know who they want to create value for before they can get the customer inputs they need to make it happen. An upfront evaluation of strategic options is crucial; otherwise, companies run the risk of failure far-

1

ther down the line. This chapter addresses the questions that managers should consider as they formulate their innovation strategies.

What Types of Innovation Are Possible?

There are four types of innovation that companies should consider for pursuit. Some are more attractive than others depending on whether the company is a start-up or an existing firm and whether it is competing in a growing or mature market.

Product innovation, or *service innovation*, which is the most common type of innovation, results from improvements that are made to existing products and services. Nearly all established companies must focus on product or service innovation or risk losing market share to a more aggressive competitor. To succeed at it, companies must discover which customer outcomes (the metrics used by customers to define the successful execution of a specific job) are being underserved and then devise and provide creative features in their products and services that do a better job of addressing those outcomes. Addressing one outcome may result in incremental improvement whereas a product that addresses many underserved outcomes is likely to produce a breakthrough improvement. For example, in 2004 the Robert Bosch Tool Corporation, known as Bosch, successfully entered the North American circular saw market with the feature-rich CS20 professional saw that addressed a number of underserved outcomes. Bosch came up with a unique idea for keeping dust off the cut line and debris away from the user's eyes. This is accomplished with a rather powerful fan that is built into the housing between the motor and the blade guard with vents aimed at the cutting path. Drawing air into the motor to cool it is an old idea. Accelerating and directing that air to clear sawdust from the cutting path and away from the user is new and helpful thinking. Bosch also removed the cord from the saw and replaced it with a socket and cord retention hook in the handle that allows the user to plug an extension cord directly into the saw. This idea has a couple of benefits for the user. It allows for easy replacement of the extension cord if the saw cuts the cord (a common occurrence), eliminating downtime and saving money. It also prevents the knot in the cord (where the traditional cord is attached to the extension cord) from catching on every edge it runs across. The Direct Connect system is designed such that it cannot come loose, enabling users to continue to lower the saw by the cord from atop a ladder. This saw includes many features that were purposefully included to address the customers' underserved outcomes, making it one of *Popular Science*'s "100 Best of What's New in 2004."

A *new market innovation* occurs when a company discovers that people (individuals or businesses) are struggling to get a job done on their own because no products exist and devises a creative product or service that enables customers to get that job done faster and cheaper than ever before; ultimately, the company creates a new market. This type of innovation is attractive to start-ups and new entrants and also outreaching established firms. New market innovation often provides the best path for revenue growth, because it does not siphon revenue away from existing product lines and ultimately results in net new growth. Under this innovation option, companies need to find "underserved jobs"—those unsatisfied tasks that may be related to ones already being handled by the companies' existing products—even if it means developing new competencies as a result. For example, the Palmz-Schatz stent developed in 1994 by Cordis Corporation was a market innovation in the field of angioplasty because it was a new, high-margin product that enabled doctors specializing in intervening heart procedures, to get a job done that they struggled with when performing the angioplasty procedure—significantly reducing restenosis (the recurrence of a blockage). This product gave them a new and profitable product line. The PC, the cell phone, and, more recently, the wireless network are also examples of new market innovations.

Operational innovation happens when a company discovers inefficiencies in a business operation and works to address those inefficiencies through creative solutions. This type of innovation typically appeals to companies in a commodity business, a mature market, or in other markets where product or service innovation is proving difficult. Operational innovation often requires companies to rethink their value chains and reconstruct them in ways that cut costs and waste; that often means making massive investments in infrastructure. To succeed at this type of innovation, companies must understand all the outcomes employees and customers are trying to achieve when engaged in a customer/company interaction— the manufacture, purchase, or distribution of a product. Armed with this information, companies can then devise breakthrough process improvements that result in new, low-cost business models. Dell, for example, successfully achieved operational innovation in the computer industry by cutting out the middleman with their "buy direct" approach. Progressive Insurance cut out claims-handling inefficiencies by cutting checks at the scene of an accident. Wal-Mart redefined retail with breakthrough improvements in procurement, warehousing, inventory tracking, and sales. And Toyota created a super-advanced production system that led to the speedy customization of their automobiles. Any business that comprises complex and inefficient business processes is well suited for operational innovation. The pharmaceutical industry, for instance, could benefit from this strategy; the sector's drug-discovery process currently takes nearly fifteen years and an average of $800 million to produce a successful new drug.

Disruptive innovation, as made popular by Harvard Business School professor Clayton M. Christensen, results when a company uses a new technology to disrupt the prevailing business model in an existing market that is filled with overserved customers. This approach to innovation is different. The other three approaches to innovation start with a focus on the customers' outcomes; the technology is created in response. In contrast, with disruptive innovation, the technology exists, and the company is in search of a customer and an opportunity. Disruptive innovation is much more difficult to systematize because there is no guarantee that the technology a company has in hand addresses any particular underserved outcome in any market—and trying to find one can be a tedious and expensive process. Nonetheless, many companies (especially those far back in the value chain, such as raw-material and chemical producers) are forced to follow this growth path as they are constantly trying to grow by finding new markets for their core technologies.

In his book *The Innovator's Solution*, Christensen describes two approaches to disruptive innovation. The first is low-end disruption. This strategy is employed when a low-cost technology is targeted at a segment of core-market customers who are overserved with the current products and services and are willing to acquire a less costly, lower-performance product. This strategy disrupts the existing business model and provides a foundation upon which to eventually attract mainstream customers. The second approach is new-market disruption. This strategy is employed when a technology is targeted at a new set of customers (nonconsumers) who do not have the skill or wealth needed to acquire and use available products (if any exist).[1]

The eight-step outcome-driven innovation process defined in *What Customers Want* is applicable to each innovation option. The process works in each case because the objective is always the same: to uncover and address opportunities, whether those opportunities are underserved jobs (new market innovation) or underserved outcomes (product or operational innovation). The process for disruptive innovation is slightly different in that it first requires a company to decide in which market they want to introduce a technology. The company must ascertain in which market the technology will address overserved jobs and enable the creation of a new, low-cost business model. Once this decision is made, the opportunities can be validated, and the solution can be refined using the same eight-step approach.

---

1. Clayton M. Christensen and Michael E. Raynor, *The Innovator's Solution: Creating and Sustaining Successful Growth* (Boston, MA: Harvard Business School Press, 2003), 43–49.

What Growth Options Should Be Considered?

When it comes to product, service, new-market, and disruptive innovation, companies have several growth options. To assist in understanding the ramifications of choosing one option over another and to help companies crystallize their innovation strategies, we have created a customer-jobs matrix. It defines four common growth options that companies should consider when setting their innovation strategies. The options are based on targeting consumers or nonconsumers and new or existing jobs. As shown in the Figure 1.1, Customer-Jobs Matrix, companies can help current users of a specific product or service get the associated job done better; help current users of a specific product get other related jobs done; help

Figure 1.1   Customer-Jobs Matrix

	Existing Customer	New Customer
New Job(s)	Devise product or service innovations that help customers get more jobs done—often ancillary or related jobs	Devise product or service innovations that help new customers do a job that nobody is doing yet; no product exists
Current Job(s)	Devise product or service innovations that help customers get a job done better	Devise product or service innovations that help new customers do a job that others are already doing

new customers do a job that others are already doing; or help new customers do a job that nobody is doing yet.

Get a Job Done Better

More than 80 percent of companies' innovation initiatives are designed to improve existing products and services that already have an established customer base. To succeed here a company must be able to uncover their customers' underserved outcomes and address them. If an initiative is successful, the resulting innovation will help a company's customers get a specific job done faster, more conveniently, safer, or cheaper than before. Cell phones from Nokia, Samsung, and Motorola; financial services offerings from Charles Schwab and Merrill Lynch; and circular saws from DeWalt, Bosch, and Makita are all examples of products or services that have an existing customer base, are focused on specific jobs, and can be systematically improved by focusing on the customer's underserved outcomes. This option is referenced in the lower-left quadrant in the Customer-Jobs Matrix.

Get More Jobs Done

Companies may know the primary job customers are trying to get done with a specific product, but to find new growth opportunities, companies often need to determine which ancillary or related jobs customers want to complete in those same circumstances and enhance the existing product to help customers get those jobs done as well. Companies that succeed here must capture job-related information from customers (not outcomes), figure out which of those jobs are underserved, and then address them. For instance, the MP3-playing function of Apple's iPod lets customers listen to music, but Apple pulled ahead of the competition because the iPod also enabled users to address several other ancillary jobs that Apple discovered customers were trying to get done such as buy music, store and organize music files, and share songs. All of these ancillary jobs were previously underserved and represented opportunities for growth. This option is referenced in the upper-left quadrant in the Customer-Jobs Matrix.

Help New Customers Do a Job That Others Are Already Doing

Under this innovation growth option, companies focus on creating innovations that target nonconsumers—individuals who want to get a job done but can't because the products available for doing the job are either expensive or require specialized skills. By targeting these nonconsumers, companies often create new markets. When Canon entered the copier market, for example, it targeted those customers who wanted to use a copier but did not want to go to a centralized copy center to get the job done. Because they were able to understand the outcomes of these new users, they were successful in delivering a product that helped them get the job done. Thus was born the market for personal copiers. And when LifeScan entered the health-care market, it targeted customers who wanted to monitor their blood-glucose levels but did not want to go to a doctor's office or a hospital for testing. Understanding their outcomes led to the successful birth of the market for personal blood-glucose test kits.

Indeed, this innovation option is quite popular in the health-care field, where the objective is often to create products and services that can be used by less-skilled people in a less-centralized location. Medical innovations have allowed cardiologists to treat heart disease with angioplasty balloons and stents, taking business away from heart surgeons who specialized in open-heart surgery, and have given people the ability to whiten their own teeth in the privacy of their homes, taking business away from dentists who performed this procedure in their offices. Other industries can do the same following the same principles. This option is referenced in the lower-right quadrant in the Customer-Jobs Matrix.

Help New Customers Do a Job Nobody Is Doing Yet

Under this innovation option, a company seeks to create a new product or service that is aimed at helping customers get a job done, where no product or service is currently available. In this situation potential customers may be using homemade or piecemeal solutions, but no formal product or service is currently available—the market does not yet exist. Many software products such as tax preparation, note taking, and customer-relationship management software, along with a host of hardware products such as the phonograph, telephone, and television all fall into this innovation growth option. To find opportunities for new market creation, a company must select a population to investigate (retirees, teenagers, or a particular ethnic group, for instance) and determine what jobs the people in that demographic are trying to get done or would like to get done, but can't accomplish today. This option is referenced in the upper-right quadrant in the Customer-Jobs Matrix.

Where in the Value Chain Should We Focus to Maximize Value Creation?

Once a company decides which innovation path and growth strategy to follow, it must then decide where in the value chain to look to maximize value creation. In the case of product innovation, for example, a company must decide whether to focus on the end user, the purchaser, the channel partner, the OEM, or some other relevant customer. If the company is following an operational innovation growth path, it must decide whether to focus on internal customers, external customers, or both. For instance, human resource managers may be the target customers in an initiative aimed at streamlining the hiring process while both customers and distribution managers may be the target of an initiative aimed at reinventing the distribution process. Making this decision is important because managers must know for whom they want to create value and who to physically contact in order to get the necessary customer inputs—the metrics they use to define the successful execution of a job. When making these decisions, companies commonly make the following three mistakes, any one of which can derail the innovation process.

The company does not consider the end user directly. Companies, especially OEMs and firms that sell only into channels, commonly fail to consider the end user as a target customer, particularly when the end user is not necessarily the primary purchaser of a product or service. In business-to-business situations, for instance, a company engaged in an innovation initiative may be tempted to talk only to the buyer or purchaser. IBM's PC division, in its earlier days, for example, would focus on getting customer requirements from channel partners (remember Computerland) rather than end users—after all IBM had a relationship with the channel partner, not the end user. They also mistakenly thought that the channel partner could give them any customer inputs they needed; after all, the channel partner had a relationship with the customer. What they found, however, was that channel partners are only qualified to provide their own cost-related outcomes, such as "increase our margins" or "increase our inventory turns," which although interesting do not reveal how customers measure value when getting a job done. If a company was to talk only with channel partners and purchasers, it may begin to think it is in a commodity market, competing only on price, when, in fact, the product may be far from commodity status. The paint division at Rohm and Haas Company, for example, discovered many opportunities in the paint market by talking to the users rather than the buyers of paints for commercial projects. Companies should focus first on the end user, particularly improving the end user's ability to get a job done, and then consider the buyer or channel as a secondary customer who is mostly concerned with price. Only the end user can legitimately provide the inputs that are needed to improve an existing product or to create a whole new one.

The company doesn't consider all relevant customers for innovation. Companies that are far back in the value chain (such as producers of raw materials or semiconductors that sell to OEMs) and those that sell directly to the end user (such as makers of computer hardware and software) often don't take the time to consider all relevant customers for innovation and therefore fail to capture or consider their inputs. In the case of companies that are far back in the value chain, they often talk with only the OEMs; they fail to directly consider the outcomes of purchasers or end users. As a result, they remain isolated in the value chain and must rely on the OEMs and others to help them figure out what customers want. For their part, the OEMS and others in the value chain are struggling to make this happen, because they, too, tend to capture the wrong customer inputs. Companies that are far back in the value chain should actively identify customers' outcomes throughout the value chain, thereby making themselves more knowledgeable and more valuable to the OEM and others in the value chain.

In the case where companies sell directly to end users, they often fail to consider *secondary*, but still critical, customers in the value chain. A printer manufacturer designing a new networked printer, for example, may focus on end users' requirements, but not on Information Technology (IT) directors' outcomes related to printer management and administration. A manufacturer of medical devices may focus on creating innovative products for physicians but neglect to consider nurses' desired outcomes or the hospital administrator's inputs. It is important to consider all relevant customers in the value chain. Businesses that overlook important constituents increase their risk of failure.

The company lets one customer speak for another. To formulate effective innovation growth strategies, companies must correctly determine who in the value chain makes the most important judgments about value and go to that source *directly* to understand what metrics they use to judge value. Often, companies take shortcuts and let their immediate customers, such as an OEM or a channel partner collect, interpret, and provide them with the requirements of others in the value chain. Companies that have a strong channel partner, such as makers of appliances or power tools, for example, may not talk to end users directly. Instead, they may accept the channel partner's list of end-user requirements as gospel, incorrectly assuming the channel partner has a good handle on what customers want. Unfortunately, the channel partner is unlikely to have the needed customer inputs as it makes the same mistakes in collecting good customer inputs as everyone else. (We'll talk more about these mistakes in Chapter 2).

Companies also like to rely on their sales forces for customer information, letting them speak for the customer—often another big mistake. Companies often believe that because the sales team is close to the customers, the sales people must know what customers want. But salespeople invariably talk about customer requirements as "solutions" and "specifications"—not as outcomes. They may know what solutions the customers are requesting and feel adamant in their position, but they, more so than others in the organization, can unintentionally mislead the rest of the organization with such feedback. Let the salespeople do what they do best: sell. When it comes to collecting information about customer requirements, let trained professionals go directly to the sources.

How Do We Handle Multiple Constituents with Potentially Conflicting Outcomes?

Companies often hesitate to consider multiple customers in the value chain when devising their innovation strategies. Doing so would add complexity to the process, executives think. Instead, companies limit the number of constituents they consider, simplifying the effort, but adding unnecessary risk to the innovation process. A critical objective of the innovation process is to discover as many opportunities for value creation as possible, so it's advantageous for businesses to consider multiple constituents and their underserved outcomes when devising their innovation strategies. When trying to come up with new products and services, an auto insurance provider, for instance, may want to consider the desired outcomes of the insured, the insurance agent, the agency owner, and those who handle auto repairs. Software developers may want to consider the desired outcomes of end users, purchasers, IT administrators, and corporate executives. Manufacturers of health-care products and services should consider the desired outcomes of patients, care providers, hospital administrators, buying groups, insurers, employers, Medicare, and other federal agencies. Once such information has been collected and analyzed, companies can discover opportunities across all constituents and then prioritize the weighting of each constituent's inputs.

Summary

Companies have several factors to consider when formulating their innovation strategies. They must first determine what type of innovation initiative to pursue: product or service innovation, new market innovation, operational innovation, or disruptive innovation.

The option chosen will depend on the organization's particular market situation and circumstances.

Companies must also determine which jobs to address and whether to target current consumers or nonconsumers. Here again, they have four options: help consumers get a specific job done better, help consumers get more jobs done, help nonconsumers get a job done that others are already doing, or help nonconsumers get a job done that nobody is doing yet. Although most companies routinely focus on helping customers get a specific job done better, the other three options often represent unique opportunities for growth and innovation.

Companies must also decide where in the value chain to focus their value-creation energy. They may target the end user, the buyer, the channel partner, the OEM, or someone else in the value chain. Companies often make three mistakes when choosing where to focus. They focus on the wrong customer, often excluding the end user from consideration; they exclude an important customer when more than one constituent should be considered; and they accept secondhand information about customer requirements.

Before a company can figure out what customers want, it must first decide for whom and how it wants to create value. Once these decisions are made, the data collection process can begin.

Capturing Customer Inputs

Silence the "Voice of the Customer"— Let's Talk Jobs, Outcomes, and Constraints

- *Why should companies gather customer requirements?*
- *What three issues plague the requirements-gathering process?*
- *What types of data do companies commonly collect from customers?*
- *What customer inputs are needed to master the innovation process?*
- *What methods should companies use to obtain the necessary information?*
- *How do you know which of the three types of inputs you should capture?*

The second step in the outcome-driven innovation process is to obtain from customers the information that is needed to discover opportunities and to create valued product or service solutions. In other words, it is to obtain the customer's "requirements." Getting the right customer inputs is essential to success because it removes variability from and adds discipline and predictability to each subsequent step in the innovation process—from the identification of opportunities, all the way to product evaluation and positioning. When using traditional "voice of the customer" methods for data collection, the needed customer inputs are rarely captured. New thinking and new methods for data collection are needed, and they are the subjects of this chapter.

Why Should Companies Gather Customer Requirements?

For a company to innovate, it must create products and services that let consumers perform a job faster, better, more conveniently, and/or less expensively than before. To achieve this objective, companies must know what outcomes customers are trying to achieve (what metrics they use to determine how well a job is getting done) and figure out which technologies, products, and features will best satisfy the important outcomes that are currently underserved.

Keep in mind, when we talk about capturing customer requirements, we are not talking about getting customer feedback on a product or service idea, concept, or prototype; that process is more about concept evaluation than requirements gathering. Rather, we are talking about understanding what metrics customers use to determine value when getting a job done—and obtaining this information in advance of devising or evaluating any product ideas and concepts. In our proposed outcome-driven paradigm, companies capture the necessary customer information and use it to guide them in the creation of valuable products or services. They do not brainstorm a range of ideas and test them with customers to see which ones consumers like best. While the latter practice is common, it is often the cause of product failures.

What Three Issues Plague the
Requirements-Gathering Process?

Despite improvements that have been made in the requirements-gathering process over the years, three issues still remain.

First, a standard definition of "requirements" still does not exist—even some twenty years into the customer-driven movement, in which companies have focused on understanding the "voice of the customer." When companies talk about customer requirements, they talk about customer needs, wants, solutions, benefits, ideas, outcomes, and specifications, and they often use these terms synonymously. Most managers would probably agree that the goal of innovation is to devise a product or service that their customers will deem valuable according to their individual criteria. So the real question is, "What criteria do customers use to measure value?"

To date, there has been little formal effort made by companies, academics, or others to define the types of information customers offer when stating their requirements, and what type of information is needed by product development groups and marketing staff to effectively create, position, and sell breakthrough products and services.

A requirement is something that customers want or need, so, arguably, solutions, specifications, and benefits could all be considered requirements. But certain types of information about customer requirements are more valuable than others to companies. To help bring clarity and objectivity to the innovation process, we need to first create a common language around the different types of information about customer requirements.

Second, companies delude themselves into thinking they are obtaining the data they need from customers—but they are not. In a study we conducted with 270 business executives in a wide range of small, medium, and large companies across many industries, we found that 72 percent of the marketing and development managers interviewed were very satisfied with their company's ability to capture customer requirements. Given this perception, it is difficult for many managers to accept that the root cause of many failed product and service initiatives is their *inability* to capture the types of customer inputs needed to successfully manage innovation. Indeed, all our studies over the past twenty years indicate that there exists a large discrepancy between the types of information companies use as inputs into the innovation process and the types of information they need. When companies are collecting information from customers, they are assuming the customers' statements are the inputs they need to successfully innovate. Unfortunately, this assumption is dead wrong. In fact, using these anecdotal inputs often causes the failures managers are so fervently trying to avoid.

As it turns out, the "voice-of-the-customer" approach to innovation is fraught with ambiguity. In a typical requirements-gathering situation, companies meet with or observe customers to ascertain their wants and needs. For their part, customers are perfectly willing to share their thoughts, but they are not aware of the types of information the company needs to create valuable products. To make matters worse, the interviewer rarely knows what types of data are needed, so he or she lets the customers state their requirements in a language that is convenient and meaningful to them. The interviewer and the company then simply accept the customers' statements as requirements, which are then used as inputs into the innovation process. The blind lead the blind—and then it gets worse. The customers' imprecise statements are then translated into more "useful" terms by marketing and development teams, so the already questionable feedback becomes even more so.

In our work with many of the world's leading-edge manufacturing and service organizations, we have found that customers tend to state (and managers tend to capture) four types of information during the requirements-gathering process: solutions, design specifications, customer needs, and customer benefit statements. Technically, these are all customer requirements. Some of them may even be useful for certain business purposes. But none of them will help a company successfully create new products and services or help the company transform its innovation activities into a systematic and manageable business process.

And third, companies spend considerable time debating the methods used to capture customer information rather than focusing on collecting the right kind of information. As part of the customer-driven movement, it has become common for companies to conduct one-on-one customer interviews; focus groups; company visits; and/or contextual, ethnographic, or anthropological research in hopes of understanding the "voice of the customer." Practitioners and academics debate which method of customer research yields the best results. But, truly, the method matters less than the types of data sought during the process. The needed data can be captured using any of the above methods, but it can only be captured when a company knows what type of information they are looking for.

What Types of Data Do Companies Commonly Collect from Customers?

In the course of gathering customer requirements, companies typically collect the following types of data.

Solutions

Many customers offer their requirements in the form of a solution to a problem. Often, customers will describe the physical or tangible features they want to see in the products or services they use. For instance, customers may tell a razor manufacturer that they want a rubberized handle or a lubrication strip on the razor head. Each of these statements represents a possible solution to a problem the customer faces. But most customers are not technologists, engineers, or scientists. They do not always have the best solutions, which means their suggestions may lead to products and services that ultimately disappoint them. Customers also do not know how the features they are requesting will affect other, possibly more important, dimensions of the product. Again, ultimately they may not like a version of the product that incorporates their requested features. Such customer feedback also can inhibit the company from looking beyond what its customers are requesting—a practice that leads to the creation of "me-too" rather than breakthrough products and services.

This is not to say that companies should not consider customer ideas—they should. But when capturing customer requirements, managers must be looking for the criteria customers use to measure the value of a product or service—not their ideas about the product or service itself. The razor manufacturers, for instance, should realize that users who ask for a lubrication strip are really trying to "minimize the number of nicks when shaving." A lubrication strip is just one way in which this criterion could be satisfied.

Specifications

Customers often focus on product specifications, giving interviewers detailed instructions on particular design characteristics: size, weight, color, shape, look, or feel. Razor users may request "a wider handle" or "a lighter weight" or "a sleek look." Again, by accepting this input from customers, companies assume that the customer knows the best solution—which is often not the case. A wider handle, for example, may have been requested to prevent the razor from slipping out of the user's hand while shaving. Although a wider handle may be helpful in solving the problem, a better option might be a regular-size handle with a ribbed, rubberized grip. Although this type of feedback may be appropriate in certain situations (among government contractors, for instance), accepting specifications as customer inputs inherently prevents engineers and designers from using their creative skills to devise breakthrough products and services.

Needs

Customers' needs are usually expressed as high-level descriptions of the overall quality of a product or service. They are typically stated as adjectives and inherently do not imply a specific benefit to the customer. For instance, customers commonly say they want a product or service to be "reliable," "effective," "robust," "dependable," or "resilient." Razor users may want the product to be "durable and strong." Although these simple statements provide some indication as to what customers are looking for, they have one major drawback. They are imprecise statements open to interpretation and present designers, developers, and engineers with the impossible task of figuring out just what customers really mean by "durable" or "strong." If engineers faced the task of making a razor more "durable," would they try to make the blade last longer, resist bending, or withstand constant moisture? Would any of these actions satisfy the customer's true measure of "durable?"

Because these inputs are imprecise, they leave too much to chance. This often leads to frustration and friction between the marketing and development departments. Marketing believes it is providing product developers with customer requirements, and developers believe they are receiving useless information—which from their perspective, they are. Good customer input must be concise, actionable, and measurable.

Benefits

Customers often use benefits statements to describe what value they would like a new product or service feature to deliver. They often use words like "easy to use," "faster," or "better." A razor user may want "a better shave," "an easy cleanup," or "a faster shave." These statements may be useful for marketing-communication purposes, but, again, they present designers and engineers with ambiguous information that can't be measured or acted upon.

In one study we conducted with Motorola cell phone users, for example, we found there were twenty-one different ways in which customers defined "easy to use." Their desired outcomes included, "minimizing the time it takes to look up a needed phone number," "minimizing the likelihood of calls being made by inadvertently hitting the keypad," and "minimizing the time it takes to dial a number without looking at the keypad." In each of those situations, "easy to use" takes on a different meaning and has different implications for designers seeking to improve or extend the product. Without understanding exactly what is meant, and which measures of value are most important to customers, managers run the risk of focusing on the wrong opportunities and making the wrong design decisions.

Managers must be aware of the types of information they are obtaining when listening to the "voice of the customer." Many firms unknowingly capture a combination of all these types of information and attempt to use them all—adding to the confusion. What many managers fail to recognize is that none of these types of inputs provide developers, engineers, marketers, and others with the information they need to devise breakthrough solutions and transform the innovation process into a predictable discipline. As we shall demonstrate, being customer-driven is just not good enough to ensure success—companies must become *outcome-driven*.

What Customer Inputs Are Needed to Master the Innovation Process?

To execute their innovation processes successfully, companies must obtain three distinct types of data. They must know which *jobs* their customers are trying to get done (that is, the tasks or activities customers are trying to carry out); the *outcomes* customers are trying to achieve (that is, the metrics customers use to define the successful execution of a job); and the *constraints* that may prevent customers from adopting or using a new product or service. These three data sources represent the primary means by which companies can create new and significant customer value: by helping customers perform ancillary jobs, new jobs, or more jobs; by improving customers' chances of getting a specific job done to satisfaction; and by removing obstacles that prevent customers from doing a job at all. A cell-phone manufacturer, for instance, can achieve growth by enabling users to get driving directions or play games online (both are ancillary jobs), by minimizing the time it takes to power up the device or preventing the likelihood of errors while dialing (making it easier for users to get a specific task done), and by improving service-area ranges (overcoming constraints to use). Let's examine more closely these three types of information.

Jobs to Be Done—a Key Factor For Growth

In both new and established markets, customers (people and companies) have jobs that arise regularly and need to get done. To get the job done, customers seek out helpful products and services. A man who needs to shave every day may purchase a razor blade and shaving cream, or he may buy an electric razor and some aftershave lotion. A woman executing a similar hair-removal process may purchase lotions or waxing strips to get the job done. As another example, a person who wants to bolster his or her family's financial security may purchase an insurance policy or an options contract for protection. In each case, the customer seeks out products and services to help get a specific job done.

Knowing what job a product or service is designed to perform is fundamental to the company's and the product's success—not to mention the customer's success at getting the job done. Less obvious, however, are the growth possibilities that may result from knowing what other supporting or related jobs customers are trying to get done, besides the primary job. Razor users may want not only to remove hair but also to "prevent dry skin" or "prevent wrinkles and age spots" or "stop bleeding when nicked." People who have MP3 players may want not only to listen to music but also to learn the words to a song, learn more about an artist, or find out when the artist will be performing locally.

Breakthrough products and services often address these ancillary and related jobs. Take Apple's iPod, a portable MP3 player that not only lets users listen to music but also enables them to download songs (legally) and organize their music libraries. Even though the iPod is considerably more expensive than MP3 players from other vendors, Apple has quickly gained dominance in the portables market by combining complementary products and services and by helping users perform jobs outside of just listening to music.

Similarly, some beverage producers are putting out products that not only satisfy thirst but also give users the vitamins, nutrients, and herbs they need to improve their mental and/or physical performance. SoBe Beverages, Red Bull Energy Drink, and Glacé au Vitaminwater all address the related functional jobs customers are trying to perform such as staying focused, working out, recovering from exercise, and trying to stay awake while also quenching their thirst. These and other similarly enhanced beverages now account for a sizable percentage of total beverage sales in the United States, and the market is expected to grow to $24 billion in sales in 2005.

Customers are often trying to perform multiple tasks simultaneously. But companies tend to focus their products and services on performing a single task; to address ancillary as well as primary jobs would require them to develop new or different competencies or to cross organizational boundaries—something they may not believe they are prepared to do, financially or culturally. Developing new competencies may require different skill sets and greater capital investments, but companies can reap significant dividends by addressing *all* the jobs customers are trying to get done under a given set of circumstances.

We have found that there are three different types of jobs that customers are often trying to get done in a given circumstance: functional jobs and personal and social jobs (two types of emotional jobs). These types of jobs are summarized in Figure 2.1. When purchasing an automobile, for example, a woman may want to be able to transport children from one location to another (functional job), but she may also want to feel successful (personal job) and be perceived as attractive by others (social job). A mom throwing a party for her child may want to arrange the party (functional job), but she may also want to feel loved by her child (personal job) and be perceived as a good mom by the other moms (social job). Functional jobs define the tasks people seek to accomplish, personal jobs explain the way people want to feel in a given circumstance, and social jobs clarify how people want to be perceived by others. All are relevant

Figure 2.1 Types of Jobs

Job to Be Done		
Functional Jobs	Emotional Jobs	
	Personal	Social

in creating customer value and should be considered as part of the data-collection effort.

Desired Outcomes—Metrics That Drive Innovation

Customers want to get more jobs done, but they also want to be able to do specific tasks faster, better, or cheaper than they can currently. To define just what "faster" or "better" means, companies must be able to capture from customers the set of metrics—measures of value, if you will—that define how they want to get the job done and what it means to get the job done perfectly. These metrics are the customers' *desired outcomes.*[1]

Let's look at the circular saw example mentioned in the last chapter. Here Bosch found that customers want to:

- Minimize the amount of kick that occurs when starting the saw
- Increase the likelihood that the blade will begin cutting precisely on the cut line
- Minimize the amount of time the cut line is blocked from view when making a cut
- Minimize the amount of pressure that must be exerted to keep the saw flat on the cutting surface
- Minimize the likelihood that the blade guard will snag the material
- Minimize the likelihood of the cut going off track when approaching the end of the material/cut
- Minimize the frequency with which the cord gets in the way of the cut path

---

1. Anthony W. Ulwick, "Turn Customer Input into Innovation," *Harvard Business Review* (January 2002), 91–97.

- Minimize the frequency with which the cord (end plug) gets caught on the material
- Minimize the frequency with which the blade binds
- Increase the number of cuts that can be made with a single blade
- Minimize the amount of damage a worn or dirty table inflicts on the material when a cut is being made
- Minimize the amount of dust/debris that is generated by the saw

These are just a few of the eighty or so outcomes they captured from customers. For most jobs, even those that may seem somewhat trivial, there are typically 50 to 150 or more desired outcomes— not just a handful. Companies must capture information about *all* the desired outcomes for the jobs their products and services address because you never know which may be underserved.

The thinking behind outcome-driven innovation is analogous to the Six Sigma initiatives that companies use to improve their internal business processes: for every process, there is a set of metrics that can be used to determine whether it has been successfully executed. With the right metrics in hand, managers can establish programs that, over time, will control process variability and ensure perfect execution. In a similar fashion, for every job customers are trying to get done, there is a set of metrics that can be used to determine how well that job is being executed when using a specific product. If a job is executed well according to a customer's individual measures of performance, the customer will consider the job done perfectly and the product will be well perceived.

There are two key differences, however, between improving internal business processes and helping customers get a job done better than before. First, when focused on innovation, companies need to collect metrics that relate to the job or the process that the *customer* is trying to get done, not an internal process that the company needs to accomplish. And second, these metrics *must* be defined by the customer, not by people within the company. There's the rub: customers do not naturally share the metrics they use to judge the value of a product or service. So managers need to engage customers in a conversation that is designed to extract the customers' desired outcomes. Although this represents a sharp departure from traditional requirements-gathering practices, it is not an impossible task. Trained interviewers can extract from customers their desired outcomes—regardless of whether the data is collected through personal or group interviews, focus groups, or anthropological research. In fact, in a typical one-hour interview, it is possible to capture between twenty and thirty desired outcomes from a single customer. The captured outcomes (again, totaling between 50 and 150 statements) collectively represent the set of performance measures that define the successful execution of a particular job or process. This point has important downstream implications: if a company knows how its customers value a product's ability to help them get a particular job done, then any proposed product idea (concept or design) can be evaluated against those measures. As we will show in later chapters, companies can quantify the amount of value a proposed product can possibly deliver, thus making it possible for them to predict which ideas will succeed and which will fail.

Before we start capturing outcomes from customers we often begin to dissect the job into its process steps so we know where to look to capture customer information. This results in a clear understanding of the customer's value model. In the Bosch circular saw example, as shown in Figure 2.2, the job of cutting wood is broken down into distinct process steps such as planning the cut, adjusting the saw, and making the cut.

To fill in the customer value model, managers must capture the customers' desired outcomes in a precise format for each stage of the job so development and marketing staffers can use the information throughout the subsequent stages of the innovation process. Desired outcomes, as shown in Figure 2.3, typically state a direction of improvement (minimize or increase); contain a unit of mea-

Figure 2.2   Customer Value Model

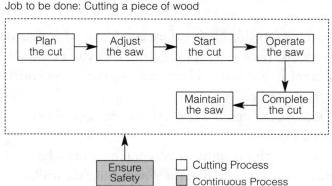

sure (number, time, frequency, likelihood); and state what outcome is desired.

Rohm and Haas found that house painters had nearly one hundred outcomes, including the following:

• Minimize the amount of paint wasted due to over-purchase (leftover paint that cannot be used on another job)
• Minimize the time it takes to protect the adjacent surfaces—window frames, baseboards, and electrical fixtures
• Minimize the time it takes to repair the surface defects—cracks, holes, and dents in walls; caulking seams—prior to painting

Figure 2.3   Dissection of an Outcome

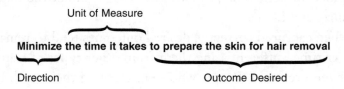

- Minimize the amount of paint wasted when it is poured from one container to another—roller pans, smaller cans, and sprayers
- Minimize the likelihood of excessive paint dripping down the painted surface and creating drip marks and ropes on walls
- Minimize the likelihood of the applicator leaving marks on the painted surface
- Minimize the number of coats that are needed to cover the old surface color
- Minimize the likelihood of contaminants—bugs, dirt, and other paint—sticking to the painted surface while it is drying
- Minimize the likelihood of damaging the new painted surface when removing the tape
- Minimize the likelihood that the finished surface will be damaged when an undesirable mark—fingerprints, crayon marks, and scuff marks—is removed

You'll notice that these outcome statements all start with "minimize." Years ago, we tried to be more colorful and used a combination of words to denote "minimize"—for instance, "reduce" and "eliminate" and "prevent." But when we asked customers to rate the importance and satisfaction levels of specific outcomes, we found that the word used to introduce the statement affected the way the statement was rated, introducing unwanted variability into the process. For example, customers may think it is important to "minimize the amount of wasted paint," but they may not find it as important to "eliminate the amount of wasted paint." Words such as "eliminate" and "prevent" imply a target value of zero, when, in fact, complete elimination may not be that critical. To avoid unwanted variability, we settled on just two words to introduce the statement: minimize and increase.

When captured correctly, desired outcomes tend to remain stable over time, differentiating them from other types of stated customer requirements. People who were cleaning their teeth back in the 1950s, for example, wanted to minimize the time it took to remove food from hard-to-reach places and minimize the likelihood of gum irritation—just as they do today and will in the future. Desired outcomes have this unique quality because they are fundamental measures of performance that are inherent to the execution of a specific job. They will be valid metrics for as long as customers are trying to get that job done. Consequently, knowing what outcomes customers are trying to achieve gives companies short-term as well as long-term direction in selecting ideas and technologies to pursue.

The completed customer value model defines the outcomes that customers are trying to achieve at each step of a job. In most cases a dozen or so outcomes define success at each step. In the Bosch circular saw example, as shown in Figure 2.4, the job of cutting wood, which is broken down into distinct process steps, has a unique set of outcomes for each step in the process. The collective set of outcomes represents the customer's value model—they are all the measures used to judge how well a job is getting done.

Figure 2.4   Customer Value Model: With Outcome Examples

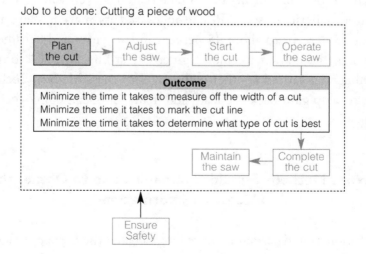

Constraints—Roadblocks to Success

Besides getting more jobs done, or a specific job done better, customers also need help overcoming the *constraints* that prevent them from getting a job done altogether or under certain circumstances. These constraints are often physical, regulatory, or environmental in nature. Companies that can find new ways to overcome these constraints can also uncover excellent growth opportunities.

Consider how Roche took over the market leadership position from Johnson & Johnson's LifeScan division in 2001 after it discovered (and addressed) a constraint that inhibited diabetes patients from using home test kits for monitoring their blood glucose. Diabetics often experience shaky hands and blurred vision when the condition is at its worst, making it impossible for them to precisely place a blood sample on a small test strip, place the strip in the device, and then interpret the reading. When they needed the device the most, these people often couldn't use it.

This constraint presented an opportunity for Roche. In 1998 the health-care products company introduced the Accu-Chek Comfort Curve. This product eliminated the need for accurate blood placement on a strip, and made it easier to place the strip in the device making it possible for people to take readings even when suffering from a diabetic episode. Roche increased its market share from about 28 percent to about 45 percent in two years and became the leader in the market for blood-glucose test kits. In 2001 Johnson & Johnson acquired another company, Inverness Medical Technology, to help gain back the lead, and many LifeScan employees lost their jobs.

What Methods Should Companies Use to Obtain the Necessary Information?

Practitioners and academics have long debated the best approach for obtaining customer data. Some tout the benefits of personal interviews and focus groups; others prefer ethnographic, anthropological, or observational research. As we said earlier, the method used for gathering customer requirements is not as important as knowing what *type* of information you want from customers (jobs, outcomes, and constraints) and working to obtain them. You just have to know what you are looking for. In many projects we conduct on behalf of companies we use a combination of personal and group interviews along with observational (following the customer around) research. Some companies prefer one approach over others. Intuit, for example, uses an ethnographic approach because the details surrounding what its customers do are often not top of mind— obvious or consciously known—for those people. Watching and quizzing customers helps Intuit ensure that jobs, outcomes, and constraints are captured. By contrast, HP, Microsoft, and other firms that boast a wide range of hardware, software, and service products, use a combination of requirements-gathering techniques.

To take a closer look at how the outcome gathering process works, let's offer as an example. AIG, the U.S.-based international insurer and financial services organization, used our methods to improve its agent services in the division that finances premium payments for businesses paying large premiums. It chose to use personal and group interviews to capture customers' desired outcomes. Over four weeks, the company interviewed thirty financing agents who use AIG's and/or a competitor's services. The interviewers focused the discussion on the activities associated with setting up and managing an insured's account. They asked the agents what they were trying to achieve when obtaining quotes, preparing agreements, obtaining approvals, managing late paying accounts, posting payments, and reinstating policies. To obtain the agents' desired outcomes, the interviewers instructed them to think through each of these activities during a typical day as they obtained quotes and offerings from different insurance companies. The interviewers asked the agents, "What makes one insurance company's offering better or worse than another, and why? And what characteristics describe the ideal service offering?" By forcing this type of discussion, the interviewers were able to prompt the agents to reveal their desired outcomes. The agents, like most customers, did not state their outcomes in a metric format. They might say, "I do not like it when I have to spend half a day reinstating a policy that was inadvertently canceled by the insurer because they mailed the bill to the wrong address." Upon hearing this statement an interviewer might say, "So this situation could be improved if you were able to minimize the time it takes to reinstate a policy that was inadvertently canceled by the insurer." The agent might say, "Exactly"—in which case, the statement would be accepted as an outcome—or "No, I just wish the insurer would stop inadvertently canceling policies." In this case, the interviewer would say, "So you want to minimize the likelihood that a policy is inadvertently canceled by the insurer," and validate that the statement is correct.

The AIG interviewers captured the agents' desired outcomes during the sessions; the interviewers typed the statements directly into a PC and validated their accuracy and completeness with the agents in real time, thereby avoiding a slog through hundreds of pages of transcripts after the fact. Each session captured three or four pages of statements that were classified as outcomes, jobs, or constraints. Any ambiguities were discussed with the agents and clarified during the session to ensure that statements would not have to be interpreted or amended later on. After several sessions, the compiled statements were consolidated so duplicate pieces of information could be removed. In the end, AIG obtained about seventy-five statements that reflected the way in which its customers measure value when setting up and managing accounts. The resulting inputs were subsequently prioritized through quantitative research and used to guide idea generation and concept evaluation, leading to the creation of a new web-based service offering that streamlined the agent's job. The new service was instituted late in 2003 and includes innovative features that are winning AIG new business.

How Do You Know Which of the Three Types of Inputs You Should Capture?

Probably the most difficult challenge in getting customer inputs is determining in advance which of the three types of customer data (jobs, outcomes, or constraints) to try to capture in a given situation. Several common situations arise.

When a company is trying to improve an existing offering in a core market, and its focus is on helping customers get a specific job done better, it should capture outcomes that are associated with the primary job users are trying to get done. AIG wanted to improve its services and help agents better set up and manage accounts. So it focused on collecting the seventy-five outcome statements related to that primary job. It placed less emphasis on uncovering other, ancillary jobs the agents were trying to get done and any constraints in the agents' way. That's because the other jobs the agents are trying to get done were not related to their interactions with AIG, and, because agents must use some service organization for premium financing, there were no constraints to use.

Other situations are a bit more complex. When the objective of the innovation initiative is to not only help the customer get a specific job done better but also determine what other jobs the customer is trying to get done in the same circumstance, the company must capture the outcomes associated with the specific job as well as other related jobs of interest. When Chiquita Brands International wanted to "reinvent" the banana, it didn't just obtain desired outcomes on the "ideal" banana; it also uncovered the jobs that customers wanted to get done when snacking. Chiquita focused on finding out why customers choose different snack foods at different times of the day and why they want snacks to contain certain ingredients. They found that many people eat bananas for sustenance; others eat bananas to relieve leg cramps. People who are trying to build muscle, however, snack on protein-rich foods, such as nuts. People who are trying to stay regular often snack on figs or prunes. By knowing what jobs people are hiring snacks for, so to speak, the company gained insight into how the banana could be redefined.

Summary

Development and marketing managers are responsible for identifying opportunities for growth, segmenting markets, conducting competitive analysis, generating and evaluating ideas, generating intellectual property, communicating value to customers, and measuring customer satisfaction. To successfully perform these activities, these managers rely on feedback from customers, which means the customer-requirements-gathering process is one of the most critical in business.

It is surprising, then, that there is such a lack of precision when it comes to capturing customer data. "Listen to the voice of the customer." That has been the marketing mantra for the past two decades, and although great strides have been made as a result of the customer-driven movement, the voice that managers are listening to needs to be silenced in order for marketing and development to be more successful. It is no longer sufficient for managers to simply gather customer requirements. Rather, they must know precisely what types of information are needed and what types of information they are collecting in order to create a more accountable model of innovation. (See Table 2.1 for a summary of the types of inputs.)

As in most disciplines, managers need a common language around which to discuss issues and build a shared understanding. The innovation process is no different. Knowing that jobs, outcomes, and constraints are desired inputs and that solutions, specifications, needs, and benefit statements hinder the successful execution of the innovation process gives managers a new language to consider when talking with external and internal customers.

Using this common language—and legitimizing desired outcomes as the metric statements needed to bring Six Sigma thinking to innovation—managers are better positioned to transform innovation into a manageable business process.

Table 2.1 Customer vs. Outcome-Driven Innovation Inputs

Customer-Driven Innovation—"Voice of the Customer"			
Solutions	**Specifications**	**Needs**	**Benefits**
The means by which a need or outcome is satisfied; often stated as a concept or a product or service feature.	A design parameter for a product or service—for instance, size, weight, color, shape, look, and feel.	A high-level descriptor of quality, often summarized with an adjective such as robust, reliable, effective, fresh, consistent and resilient.	A statement such as "easy to use" that customers utilize to describe what value they would like a new feature or solution to deliver.
Razor solutions, for example, may include:	Razor specifications, for example, may include:	Razor needs, for example, may include:	• Long-lasting • Faster shave • No-slip grip • Lower cost
• Triple blades • A rubberized handle • A lubrication strip • A more powerful motor	• A wider handle • Lightweight • A sleek look • Titanium blades	• Durable • Dependable • Sturdy • Strong	Benefit statements are often stated at a high level and do not provide the precision needed to determine just how to improve product or service performance.
Customers are rarely qualified to suggest a breakthrough solution. Giving customers the solutions they request often results in the creation of "me-too" products and services.	Designing products and services to meet customer specifications is dangerous as customers fail to consider all the design trade-off decisions that must be made.	Need statements are often vague and ambiguous, making it difficult for engineers and developers to determine precisely what to do to create customer value.	

Outcome-Driven Innovation—Jobs, Outcomes, Constraints		
Jobs Related to Removing Body Hair	**Desired Outcomes on the Job of Removing Body Hair**	**Constraints on a Product That Removes Body Hair**
• Prevent skin from drying, flaking, and peeling • Slow the skin from aging, prevent wrinkles, age spots, and so on	• Minimize the time it takes to prepare the skin for hair removal • Minimize the likelihood of nicks • Minimize the frequency with which hair must be removed • Minimize the likelihood of skin irritation	• The product must be usable with one hand • The product must not require the use of mirror
Growth results when a company helps a customer get more jobs done. Knowing which jobs are important and difficult to perform reveals target opportunities for growth.	Value can be created by helping customers get a job done better by satisfying the outcomes that are underserved.	Value can also be created by helping a customer overcome an obstacle to getting a job done in a given situation.

Today, very few employees in any firm know *all* the jobs that customers are trying to get done, *all* the outcomes they are trying to achieve, and *all* the constraints that are standing in the way of product use. Improvement is inevitable when *all* employees across a firm have access to this valuable information and are empowered and motivated to use it to create customer value.

Without the proper inputs, the innovation process will remain an art. However, those managers who know what types of information to look for (and what types to ignore) will be at the forefront of a transformation in the way that companies manage their innovation processes.

CHAPTER

Identifying Opportunities

Discovering Where the Market Is Underserved and Overserved

- *What is an opportunity?*
- *What three common mistakes are made in prioritizing opportunities?*
- *How should companies prioritize opportunities?*
- *How do you identify underserved and overserved markets?*
- *How does value migrate over time?*
- *What implications does the outcome-driven paradigm have for competitive analysis?*

The third step in the outcome-driven innovation process is to determine what jobs, outcomes, and constraints represent the best opportunities for growth and innovation. To successfully execute this process step, a company must have captured the customer inputs already and must now determine which of those jobs, outcomes, and constraints are most underserved and represent solid opportunities for improvement and which are most overserved and represent unique opportunities for cost reduction and possible disruption.

Companies struggle to define, identify, and prioritize opportunities and often inappropriately apply resources to address outcomes that are already well satisfied. The reasons for this are many. Indeed, numerous obstacles stand in the way of identifying and prioritizing opportunities. Chapter 3 is dedicated to exploring and overcoming those roadblocks.

What Is an Opportunity?

One fundamental reason companies struggle to identify opportunities is because they lack a clear definition of just what an opportunity is. *Opportunity*, like *requirement*, has been defined and redefined in so many ways that it does not have a clear meaning. Often, when managers talk about uncovering areas of opportunity, for example, they are referring to identifying new ideas, technologies, or solutions that customers may want. A razor manufacturer, for example, may believe that adding a fifth blade is a great opportunity. (When will they stop? Wasn't three good enough?) Companies believe such solutions offer opportunities for growth, but that thinking is backward.

In the outcome-driven paradigm, an opportunity for growth is defined as an outcome, job, or constraint that is underserved. An underserved outcome, in turn, can be defined as something customers want to achieve but are unable to achieve satisfactorily, given the tools currently available to them. These underserved outcomes point to where customers want to see improvements made and where they would recognize the delivery of additional value. If circular saw users, for example, think that minimizing the likelihood of the cut going off track is an important and unsatisfied outcome, then that would represent an opportunity for improvement among the 50 to 150 outcomes related to executing that job.

Underserved jobs signal potential opportunities for new markets. They are jobs that customers cannot perform satisfactorily with the tools that are currently available to them. Job-related opportunities for growth can be discovered by determining what ancillary or related jobs are underserved when a customer is using an existing product or service and by determining what jobs people are trying to get done in general. If it turns out that preventing skin dryness is an important and unsatisfied job when shaving, then customers may value a product that would help them perform that job more effectively. If it were determined that people want to wake up with fresh breath after sleeping all night, then that job might represent an opportunity for a brand new market.

Underserved constraints also represent opportunities for growth as they point out under what conditions or circumstances a customer is unable to perform a job of interest.

Outcome, job, and constraint statements provide managers with quantifiable, tangible measures along which to create new products and services. These measures represent solid opportunities for improvement and growth. When Bosch used this approach to make its entrée into the North American circular saw market, they uncovered a dozen outcome-related opportunities for improvement in a very mature market, many of which were previously unknown to their development team. This insight led to the creation of a very innovative and successful product.

Agreeing on what comprises an opportunity is the foundational first step. Having once defined opportunity, a company can then identify and prioritize the opportunities open to it.

What Three Common Mistakes Are Made in Prioritizing Opportunities?

Companies typically fail to prioritize opportunities effectively because they lack the methods needed to prioritize them. Instead, some simply focus on what is easy to complete, putting difficult tasks at the bottom of the list, regardless of what represents the best opportunity for growth. Others may focus on what an engineer finds most interesting or what a marketing manager deems to be most important. In some cases, the sales force may determine the priority based on what they most frequently hear customers request, or a company may let lead users prioritize its efforts, even though the rest of the market might have other priorities. In still other cases, a company may let its CEO or other key executive prioritize opportunities (this we find all too often). In any of those scenarios, companies must rely on opinion, intuition, and guesswork, and as a consequence they often make three common missteps: making unnecessary improvements by targeting outcomes that are already well satisfied, making improvements that satisfy unimportant outcomes, and making improvements that, while satisfying certain outcomes, inadvertently have a negative effect on other, more important outcomes.

Making improvements in areas that are already satisfied. Companies often spend years developing a competency or strength in a market and then continue to improve the products that showcase that competency. Certain printer manufacturers, for example, now produce desktop printers that churn out not five or ten, but up to fifty pages per minute. Granted, minimizing the time it takes to print out a page is an important outcome for most printer users, but just because a company can continue to make improvements in this area does not mean it should. Do people want a printer that will churn out 100 pages a minute, or was 30 pages a minute good enough? Are customers willing to pay more for 100 pages per minute? Companies have a tendency to keep making improvements in their areas of strength even though the associated outcome may already be well satisfied, even overserved. They believe they should continue making improvements because they can—after all, they are known for the competency, and more is better . . . or is it? How many blades will razor manufacturers squeeze onto a razor? How much smaller does a cell phone have to be? How much more horsepower do we need in our automobiles? Continuing to make product or service improvements that address well-satisfied or overserved outcomes can add unnecessary cost to a product, misdirect resources from real opportunities, and fail to add additional customer value.

Making improvements that satisfy unimportant outcomes. When companies focus on what *can* be done rather than what *should* be done, they often focus on an outcome that is just not that important to customers. Any improvements that are made in this area will ultimately be viewed as unnecessary. This mistake is a waste of company time and resources; worse yet, it may add unnecessarily to the cost of the product, making it less competitive. And, it takes resources away from the underserved outcomes that would result in the creation of value, adding an opportunity cost to the equation as well.

Making improvements that negatively impact other outcomes. Companies rarely know all the outcomes customers are trying to achieve, and often the improvements they make in one area end up having a negative effect on other important outcomes. This is very common when companies are busy listening to the "voice of the customer." Road warriors, for example, may say they want a smaller cell phone, but they may not have thought about how hard that tiny phone will be to use. Carpenters may request a lightweight circular saw without thinking about the fact that it will no longer have the power to get through some of the more difficult jobs. When customers make requests for new product features, they are usually focused on solving just one problem and are not thinking of how their requested solution will impact other product or service functions. In this situation, customers request new features but reject the resulting product when they realize the ramifications of their suggestions—the added feature turns out to be worthless because of the problems it causes, the new product delivers less value than the one it replaced, and the product fails.

A company must be aware of all the outcomes customers are trying to achieve so it makes the right trade-offs when devising a new product or service. Making improvements in one area without knowing what other outcomes will be impacted causes the product failures companies are trying to avoid.

How Should Companies Prioritize Opportunities?

Selecting the richest areas of opportunity from a long list of desired outcomes is critical, since chasing after those that are less promising drains resources. So, how can a company uncover and prioritize the most promising new product and service opportunities? Executives struggle with this question every day. Outcome-based research offers a surprisingly simple answer.

We find that most managers agree that an outcome that is both important and unsatisfied represents a solid opportunity for improvement and that addressing it successfully would result in a valued product or service. The best opportunities, then, spring from those desired outcomes that are important to a customer but are not satisfied by existing products and services. The question then becomes, "What method is best for discriminating between the best and worst opportunities to pursue?" To address this issue, we have developed a quantitative research method that has been proven very accurate and successful over the past eight years. To quantitatively prioritize these opportunities, companies perform outcome-driven research taking the following five steps:

1. Prepare a survey instrument (questionnaire) that states all the job, outcome, and constraint statements that have been captured from customer interviews and from screening and profiling questions.
2. Administer the survey to a statistically valid representation of the target population (often between 180 and 600 people).

3. Ask the survey participants to rate the importance of all the jobs, outcomes, and constraints using a scale of 1 to 5, where 5 means critically important and 1 means not important at all.
4. Ask the survey participants the degree to which they are satisfied with how the solutions they are using today address those jobs, outcomes, and constraints using a scale of 1 to 5, where 5 means totally satisfied and 1 means not satisfied at all.
5. Enter the results into the opportunity algorithm to determine which jobs, outcomes, and constraints are underserved and overserved.

The opportunity algorithm, shown in Figure 3.1, is a simple mathematical formula that makes it possible to discover the most promising areas for improvement. The formula states that opportunity equals importance plus the difference between importance and satisfaction, where that difference is not allowed to go below zero. The opportunities that are most important and least satisfied receive the highest priority.

The importance and satisfaction ratings for each outcome are entered into the equation to determine the level of opportunity. To see how this algorithm works, look at Table 3.1, which lists some of the many outcomes Bosch culled from carpenters, roofers, electricians, and others who use circular saws in their work. In outcome 1, users gave a very high rating (9.5) to "Minimize the likelihood of going off track when approaching the end of the cut." This rating means 95 percent of those interviewed rated the outcome a 4 or a 5 for importance. They gave a much lower score (3.2) when asked to rate the degree to which this outcome was currently being satis-

Figure 3.1 Opportunity Algorithm

Importance + *max*(Importance - Satisfaction, 0) = **Opportunity**

Table 3.1 Market Opportunity Scores for Circular Saws

Desired Outcomes	Importance	Satisfaction	Opportunity
1. Minimize the likelihood of going off track when approaching the end of the cut	9.5	3.2	15.8
2. Minimize the frequency with which the cord gets in the cut path	8.3	4.2	12.4
3. Minimize the amount of splintering that occurs when making a cut	9.5	7.5	11.5
4. Minimize the likelihood of debris blowing in the user's eyes	9.1	8.4	9.8
5. Minimize the time it takes to make bevel adjustments	5.1	1.0	9.1
6. Minimize the likelihood of getting cut when using the saw	9.0	9.2	9.0

fied. This rating means that only 32 percent of the interviewees rated this outcome a 4 or a 5 for satisfaction. Those two scores were inserted into the formula (9.5 + (9.5−3.2), yielding an opportunity score of 15.8. Outcome 3, "Minimize the amount of splintering that occurs when making a cut," was rated as important as outcome 1, but was satisfied to a much greater degree (7.5 versus 3.2). As a result, outcome 3 represents a much lesser opportunity, as indicated by its opportunity score of 11.5.

This algorithm also lets companies overcome the limitations associated with traditional gap analysis, an approach that considers only the difference between importance and satisfaction. Using gap analysis, for example, outcomes 2 and 5 (both with a gap of 4.1) would represent equal opportunities. Using the opportunity calculation, the opportunity associated with outcome 2 is 36 percent higher (12.4 versus 9.1) because of its greater importance.

It is also important to note that in the opportunity algorithm, the amount in parentheses can never be less than zero. In other words, high levels of satisfaction do not detract from importance. An outcome with an importance rating of 6.5 and a satisfaction rating of

8.5 would be put in the formula as: $6.5 + (6.5 - 8.5)$ or $6.5 + 0$, yielding an opportunity score of 6.5 rather than 4.5. This is important when making design trade-off decisions, because we must be certain that important outcomes are included in the concept evaluation process. The algorithm can theoretically result in scores that range from 0 (if both importance and satisfaction are 0) to 20 (if importance is 10 and satisfaction is 0). We have never seen these extremes in practice, as it is rare that an outcome has no importance or that a critically important outcome is not satisfied at all.

To critics, our scaling method can seem overly simple. It is true that it is simple, but it is also very effective. One key difference between outcome-driven research and traditional research methods is that the former focuses on evaluating jobs and outcomes, not solutions. Research methods that focus on solutions often require the use of complex scaling methods (such as paired comparisons, repeat-pairs techniques, balanced scales, comparative scales, constant-sum scales, graphic-rating scales, and rank-order scales) because they are trying to quantify something extremely subjective—what solutions customers like best. But at this stage in the outcome-driven paradigm the objective is not to figure out what solutions customers like best, but to figure out where the areas of opportunity lie in a market, that is, to determine which jobs and outcomes are underserved—and, as the formula shows, that can be determined quite easily. Figuring out what solutions best address those opportunities is a separate step that occurs later in the process; it will be discussed in Chapters 7 and 8.

Critics also argue that one can't subtract satisfaction from importance, that doing so is like subtracting apples from oranges. This comment typically comes from those who are well entrenched in the customer-driven paradigm and traditionally test solutions or features rather than jobs, outcomes, and constraints when conducting quantitative research. Their argument may be true when it comes to evaluating solutions, but it does not hold up when talking about jobs, outcomes, and constraints. When we ask razor users, for example, "How important is it to you that you are able to minimize the likelihood of nicks?" and "How satisfied are you with the degree to which the Schick razor you use today enables you to minimize the likelihood of nicks?" we are asking how important a certain outcome is and how well that outcome is currently satisfied. In that situation, it makes good sense to subtract satisfaction from importance, because we are looking for situations in which an outcome is important, and there is a big difference between the level of importance and the level of satisfaction. If an outcome is important and unsatisfied, it is an obvious area of opportunity.

We are also often told, "You need sample sizes of 1,000 respondents or more in order to accurately assess the priority of the opportunities." These critics do not approve of our using sample sizes that often range from 180 to 600 respondents, yet we feel that this is more than enough. All we are trying to do is to determine which of the 50 to 150 outcomes that we have identified are important and unsatisfied and which are not. We are not sticklers as to whether or not we have them in the exact order—if the second stated opportunity is really third in priority, and so on. When it comes time to target a set of opportunities (as discussed in Chapter 5), companies are likely to target the top ten or so, thereby including all the key opportunities. This is not to say that larger sample sizes may not be needed for other reasons, for example, when many subsets of the data must be analyzed.

How Do You Identify Underserved and Overserved Markets?

Once we've obtained the opportunity scores for each job, outcome, and constraint what comes next? With the experience of hundreds of projects behind us, we have established an effective approach to interpret the scores that result from using the opportunity algorithm. The algorithm reveals two complementary pieces of information: where the market is underserved and where it is overserved. We use this information to make some important targeting and resource-related decisions.

Where Is the Market Underserved?

An opportunity for improvement exists when an important outcome is underserved—that is, when it has a high opportunity score. Such outcomes merit the allocation of time, talent, and resources, as customers will recognize solutions that successfully serve these outcomes to be inventive and valuable. Given that higher opportunity scores represent better opportunities, we have devised the following set of rules:

• Outcomes and jobs with opportunity scores greater than 15 represent extreme areas of opportunity that should not be ignored. This range is denoted in the lower-right section in Figure 3.2. Outcomes with scores in this range are rare in mature markets, but common in newer markets, such as those for medical devices. Companies can also expect to see outcomes with scores this high when they employ the segmentation methods described in Chapter 4 to fine-tune where they search for opportunities.

• Outcomes and jobs with opportunity scores between 12 and 15 can be defined as "low-hanging fruit," ripe for improvement. Outcomes with scores in this range are common in many markets as products and services rarely execute a job perfectly. Here again, the segmentation methods described in the next chapter reveal a greater number of opportunities of this magnitude in certain segments of the market.

Figure 3.2 Interpreting Opportunity Scores

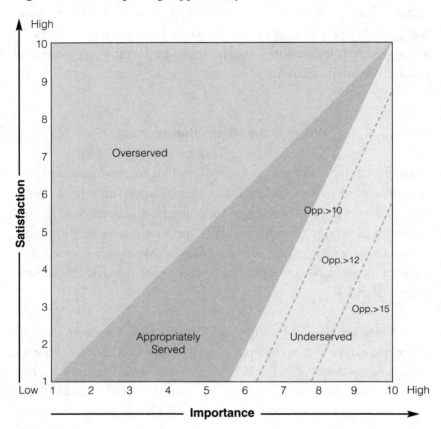

• Outcomes and jobs with opportunity scores between 10 and 12 are worthy of consideration especially when discovered in the broad market. Many such opportunities are commonly revealed even in the most mature markets.

• Outcomes and jobs with opportunity scores below 10 are viewed as unattractive in most markets and offer diminishing returns. In some less functional markets, such as those for packaging materials, however, opportunity scores in this lower range may be worthy of consideration. They are found in the upper-left section of Figure 3.2.

Where Is the Market Overserved?

Almost as important as knowing where the market is underserved is knowing where it is overserved. Jobs and outcomes that are unimportant or already satisfied represent little opportunity for improvement and consequently should not receive any resource allocation. In most markets, it is not uncommon to find a number of outcomes that are overserved—and companies that are nevertheless continuing to allocate them development resources. We say that an outcome is overserved when its satisfaction rating is higher than its importance rating. When a company discovers these overserved outcomes, it should consider the following three avenues for possible action: First, if the company is currently focusing on these overserved outcomes, those efforts should be halted. Making additional improvements in areas that are already overserved is simply a waste of resources and is likely to add cost without adding additional value. Second, if cost reduction is an important consideration in the market, then costs can be reduced by taking out costly function in areas that are overserved. For example, if a five-dollar feature can be redesigned so that it satisfies an outcome 80 percent as well as it does currently but for half the cost, then the company may want to make this trade-off. Third, if many overserved outcomes are discovered in a market, then the company should consider the possibility of engaging in disruptive innovation. This would mean taking out cost along multiple dimensions and creating a lower-cost business model that existing competitors would be unable to match. The concept of a low-end disruptive innovation, as described in *The Innovator's Solution*, is only possible when the customer population, or a segment of that population, is overserved.[1]

Knowing where the market is overserved and underserved helps guide a company's resource allocation, but it's not the only key to

---

1. Clayton M. Christensen and Michael E. Raynor, *The Innovator's Solution: Creating and Sustaining Successful Growth* (Boston, MA: Harvard Business School Press, 2003), 50.

success in innovation. Understanding how value migrates over time is also essential, and that too is possible using the opportunity algorithm.

How Does Value Migrate Over Time?

In *Value Migration*, Adrian Slywotzky describes how changing customer priorities are responsible for the displacement of old business models. Opportunities for improvement migrate over time in a dynamic fashion; today's big opportunity is not necessarily tomorrow's, and to succeed over the long term, companies must be able to determine exactly where opportunities exist in a market at any point in time and be the first to address them.[2] This, in essence, is the goal of innovation: to define and deliver new solutions that evolve each measure of value along its continuum, better satisfying the collective set of outcomes. Using the opportunity algorithm, it is possible to predict just where value is migrating.

Before explaining how, it is important to remember that the customers' *outcomes* are stable over time. People who shave, for example, have always wanted to minimize the number of nicks, minimize shaving time, and minimize the number of passes that must be made. These and other shaving-related desired outcomes will remain the same for years to come. What does change, however, is the degree to which these outcomes are satisfied by new technologies and product and service features. Once an outcome is well satisfied by a feature or technology, the opportunity score decreases for that outcome, and opportunities for value creation migrate to the other important, unsatisfied outcomes. If a company were to continue to focus on the same outcome, it would only lead to overserving the market along that dimension. This fundamental princi-

---

2. Adrian J. Slywotsky, *Value Migration* (Boston, MA: Harvard Business School Press, 1996), 12–24.

ple guides the dynamics of innovation. When an outcome has been satisfied, a company must either look to other outcomes to create additional value, as Bosch did on the CS20 circular saw when they added a feature that minimized the time it took to adjust the bevel cut to commonly selected settings, or to other jobs, as Apple did when they enabled the iPod to organize play lists and share music. When companies fail to look to other outcomes or jobs, they leave the door open for some other company to devise new product features, new business models, and new value propositions specifically aimed at addressing those remaining opportunities in the market—and the innovator just might be able to take over the market leadership position.

This dynamic is illustrated in Figure 3.3. An unspecified DeWalt circular saw (the model number is unspecified to protect the confi-

Figure 3.3 Dynamics of Innovation

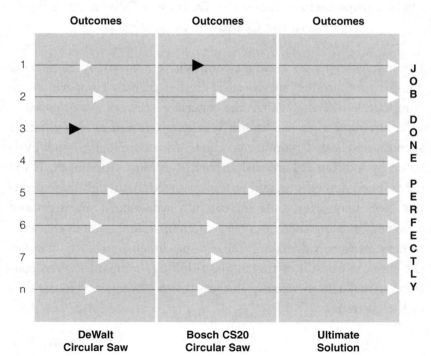

dentiality of Bosch's competitive research), represented on the far left, satisfies outcome 3 poorly; this represents the best opportunity for improvement. The Bosch CS20 circular saw, shown in the middle, addresses this opportunity with a well-crafted feature, so its satisfaction level is greatly increased and this outcome no longer represents the best opportunity for improvement. Instead, outcome 1 has become the best opportunity for improvement and should be a main consideration when creating the next-generation circular saw. Every time a new product or technology is introduced, the opportunity for value creation migrates somewhere else. To understand how this dynamic is playing out at any given time, companies must know three things: what all the customer outcomes are, which of those outcomes are important, and which are unsatisfied. With this information in hand, it is possible to see where value is migrating and to be the first to address the new opportunities with winning products.

What Implications Does the Outcome-Driven Paradigm Have for Competitive Analysis?

Companies typically conduct competitive analysis by comparing competitors' product specifications rather than by comparing each competitive offering against the criteria customers use to measure value. In many high-tech industries this is referred to as comparing speeds and feeds. Computer products, for example, are often evaluated by looking at hard disk capacity, amount of memory, DVD drive speed, screen size, and processor speed. Although these product specs may offer some insight into a product's strengths and weaknesses, using them as a basis of comparison assumes that customers measure value along these same dimensions—which is not the case. As a result of this flawed thinking, companies often continue to make improvements in areas that are overserved in the eyes of the customer.

The outcome-driven paradigm, by contrast, directs companies to keep their eyes on the job customers are trying to get done, not on their competitors' product specifications. By using the 50 to 150 desired outcomes statements as metrics against which to compare the performance of competitive products, managers can gain unique insight into how well products perform against customers' measures of value. PC manufacturers, for example, are able to see which computers are best at minimizing the time it takes to load all needed programs at start-up, which are best at minimizing the time it takes to switch from a dial-up to a local area network (LAN) connection to retrieve e-mail, and which excel at minimizing the frequency with which data is lost—all outcomes that customers value highly.

In addition, an outcome-driven competitive analysis makes it possible for a company to:

- Identify competitors' strengths and weaknesses
- Know which of its competitors' features to emulate
- Know when competitors are headed in the wrong direction and should be left to go it alone.

To illustrate these points, consider, for example, Bosch's outcome-driven competitive analysis of the circular saw market, as illustrated in Table 3.2. (To protect the company's proprietary secrets, Table 3.2 presents a fictionalization of the actual analysis. Although it does not contain the actual data, this fictionalization illustrates how Bosch's outcome-driven analysis worked.) In the column on the far left you can see nine of the eighty or so outcomes that Bosch identified as the metrics customers use to judge value. Importance (Imp), satisfaction (Sat), and opportunity (Opp) values are listed in the adjacent columns. In the three columns on the right are the satisfaction scores of three key competitors (DeWalt, Makita, and Bosch), which were captured through quantitative research with a representative sample of the population. In a blind

Table 3.2 Outcome-Driven Competitive Analysis

Desired outcomes for a circular saw	Imp	Sat	Opp	Satisfaction		
				DeWalt	Makita	Bosch
Minimize the likelihood of snagging the guard on the material	8.3	4.2	12.4	5.6	3.8	4.5
Minimize the frequency with which the cord gets in the path	8.3	5.3	11.3	5.5	4.6	5.4
Minimize the percentage of time the cut line is blocked from view	7.6	4.4	10.8	4.6	4.4	4.5
Minimize the likelihood of debris blowing in the user's eyes	8.5	6.9	10.1	6.5	7.2	7.1
Minimize the time it takes to make bevel adjustments	8.7	7.7	9.7	7.8	7.6	7.7
Minimize the likelihood that the saw will be stolen	7.5	6.1	8.9	6.3	5.9	6.1
Minimize the likelihood of the cut going off track	6.5	5.5	7.5	5.3	5.5	5.4
Minimize the time it takes to clean up	5.5	6.2	4.8	6.1	6.3	6.2
Minimize the frequency of blade change	4.4	6.7	2.1	8.8	6.4	6.7

survey, Bosch asked each survey participant which company's circular saw they used and then asked them how satisfied they were with that saw's ability to address each outcome. The results gave Bosch valuable market and competitive insights.

Identifying Competitors' Strengths and Weaknesses

Knowing what key opportunities for improvement exist in a market and who does the best and worst job of addressing each opportunity is valuable competitive information. Bosch learned that DeWalt performed best at minimizing the likelihood of snagging the guard on the material: 56 percent of DeWalt users rated the saw's ability to address this outcome a 4 or 5. Makita was the least successful at addressing this outcome: just 38 percent of Makita users were satisfied with the saw's ability to minimize the likelihood of snagging. In looking down the list of outcomes in Table 3.2, it becomes easy to see the strengths and weaknesses of each competitor. Bosch's biggest weaknesses (the areas not well addressed by the organization) are also its areas of greatest opportunity; they require immediate attention.

The information gained from this type of competitive analysis can be used to help position existing products, to understand why one competitor's product is selling better than another's, and to target the weaknesses of key competitors. It can also be used to direct the organization's communication and sales strategy to highlight the high-opportunity areas that are well served.

Knowing Which Features to Emulate

Once a company learns which competitor does best at addressing a key opportunity in the market, it can attempt to emulate that competitor. Once Bosch, for example, knows that DeWalt does the best job at minimizing the likelihood of snagging the guard on the material, then Bosch can see just what features DeWalt incorporates into their product to achieve that level of satisfaction. Bosch can then attempt to emulate that feature set or use it as a baseline from which to make additional improvements. Bosch also knows that emulating Makita's approach is not the way to go.

Knowing When to Let a Competitor Go It Alone

Companies will often follow a competitor's moves, adding to their product any new feature the competitor introduces. In the face of uncertainty, companies simply copy their competitors because they feel they must meet or beat them on a spec-by-spec basis or be left behind. A company that is thinking in terms of customer outcomes has been freed from the spec-by-spec mentality, however, and will not necessarily try to match the competition. If a company sees that a competitor's new feature addresses an outcome that is already satisfied or an outcome that is unimportant, then it knows not to follow that competitor's move. Left to go it alone, the competitor will end up with a more costly product that delivers no additional value. In the example, DeWalt overserves the outcome (minimize the frequency of blade change) with a high satisfaction score of 8.8. Bosch is not apt to follow that move because the outcome is satisfied well enough all ready. Knowing when not to follow along is the type of strategic insight that will lead to success in the long term.

Summary

Before opportunities can be addressed, they must be discovered, and before they are discovered, they must be defined. In the outcome-driven paradigm, an opportunity is defined as an outcome, job, or constraint that is important and unsatisfied given the products and services that are available today. To discover these opportunities companies employ a five-step outcome-driven research methodology:

- Prepare a survey instrument (questionnaire) that states all the job, outcome, and constraint statements that have been captured from customer interviews and from screening and profiling questions.
- Administer the survey to a statistically valid representation of the target population—often between 180 and 600 people.
- Ask the survey participants to rate the importance of all the jobs, outcomes, and constraints using a scale of 1 to 5, where 5 means critically important and 1 means not important at all.

• Ask the survey participants the degree to which they are satisfied with how the solutions they are using today address those jobs, outcomes, and constraints (here survey participants use a scale of 1 to 5 where 5 means totally satisfied and 1 means not satisfied at all).

• Enter the results into the opportunity algorithm to determine which jobs, outcomes, and constraints are underserved or overserved.

The opportunity algorithm, shown in Figure 3.1, is the mathematical formula that makes it possible to discover the most promising areas for improvement. The formula states that opportunity equals importance plus the difference between importance and satisfaction, where that difference is not allowed to go below zero.

This algorithm makes it possible to decide how resources should be allocated by showing where the market is underserved and overserved, where value is migrating over time, and what a company's strengths and weaknesses are, both in absolute terms and in terms relative to competitors. Once the opportunities are discovered, they can be addressed in ways that provide true value for customers.

Segmenting the Market

Using Outcome-Driven Segmentation to Discover Segments of Opportunity

- *What is the purpose of segmentation?*
- *How has the practice of segmentation evolved?*
- *Why are traditional segmentation methods ineffective for purposes of innovation?*
- *What is different about outcome-based segmentation?*
- *How is outcome-based segmentation performed?*
- *How does outcome-based segmentation address development and marketing challenges?*
- *How is job-based segmentation different, and when should it be used?*

The fourth step in the outcome-driven innovation process is market segmentation. For decades companies have talked about creating products and services that address the unique needs of customers in different segments of the market, yet they still struggle with the process—mainly because of problems with traditional segmentation methods. Companies realize those methods are ineffective, but what we have discovered in our work with *Fortune* 1000 companies over the past ten years is far more disturbing: today's segmentation methods drive companies to target phantom segments (groups of customers that do not really exist), resulting in the very product and service failures that companies are trying to avoid.

How can this be? For many decades it has been common practice for companies to group their customers by the types of products they buy or by their price point or to use demographic or psychographic classifications such as age, business size, comfort with technology, or level of risk aversion. These classification schemes are convenient for the company and effective for certain marketing or sales tracking purposes, but they do not generally bring together the groups of customers that offer the greatest opportunity for the company—customers that have unique underserved outcomes.

Our method, by contrast, does uncover groups of customers with unique, underserved jobs or outcomes; we think of these groups of customers as "segments of opportunity." These segments of opportunity point to new possibilities for value creation as well as to market entry points for disruptive innovation; they also reveal hard-to-find opportunities in mature markets. In Chapter 3 of *The Innovator's Solution*, Clayton M. Christensen illustrates how market categorization or segmentation schemes that are attribute-based versus outcome-based can affect the sorts of improvements that innovators are inclined to consider. This chapter provides important background on segmentation theory and describes how an outcome-driven approach to segmentation addresses the challenges faced by many firms today.

What Is the Purpose of Segmentation?

Segmentation serves a number of purposes in an organization. Customers are segmented by corporate finance groups so the company can better track financial results. Sales executives segment markets so customers are more easily targeted with advertising and marketing programs. Industry analysts segment markets so they can more easily explain industry trends and competitive movements. The methods used to segment markets for these purposes, however, are not the best methods for development and marketing to use when segmenting markets for the purpose of innovation.

Our focus here is to describe the best segmentation method for companies to use for the sole purpose of innovation—that is, for the creation of new products and services. We are not recommending these methods be used for any other purpose, nor are we suggesting that other methods are inappropriate when used in the right context. What we are saying is that there is a best way to segment markets for the purpose of innovation, and the outcome-driven methods we have developed meet the criteria we use to judge an effective approach.

When it comes to innovation, development and marketing functions encounter many challenges which can only be addressed through an effective segmentation methodology that enables the discovery of groups of customers that have a unique set of underserved or overserved outcomes. These segments of opportunity are identified using the methods described within, but, before they are described, a quick history on the evolution of segmentation and its impact on innovation is in order.

How Has the Practice of Segmentation Evolved?

Over the years, the practice of segmentation has been both defined and limited by the types of customer information that have been available to most firms. In the 1950s market segmentation was based purely on demographic characteristics such as age, geographic location, or gender because demographic information was the only type of data that was easily collected and readily available. Over time, marketing, sales, and accounting systems were designed to track and analyze data from a demographic perspective, giving these demographic-based segments a permanent home in the corporate environment.

As information technology evolved in the 1970s, so did marketers' ability to gain insight into their customer base. They developed new methods of segmentation that included not only demographic data but psychographic data as well. With information on common customer traits and attitudes toward products and services, marketers were able to produce more-specific customer profiles. As organizations installed large transaction databases and captured real-time point-of-purchase data, even more information became available to marketers. Purchase-behavior segmentation arose in response to this information flow, giving companies the ability to segment customers not only based on their age, income, and psychographic profiles, but also based on their past purchase behavior.

In the 1980s companies discovered "needs-based" segmentation. This approach was made possible by powerful computers and sophisticated clustering techniques, which allowed researchers to classify customers into segments based on what product features and benefits were most appealing to them. This approach provided managers with some helpful insights but failed to take over as the standard for segmenting markets because the segments it uncovered were often intangible and difficult to understand and target. More often than not, the "needs-based" statements used to segment markets did not really represent "needs" at all.

Today, companies often use a combination of demographic, psychographic, and "needs" data as the basis for market segmentation. Figure 4.1 provides a graphical representation of when the various types of data came to be used in market segmentation. Perhaps because segmentation schemes based on these data have been useful for sales, marketing, and accounting functions, managers have tended to overlook the schemes' unintended and often undesirable effects on the organization's ability to innovate.

Figure 4.1   Evolution of Segmentation Methodology

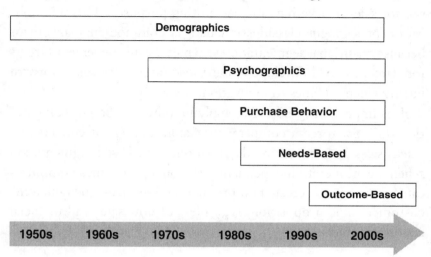

The communications company Nortel Networks, for example, which for years organized its small-business sales tracking and accounting systems around vertical industry classifications such as public services, transportation, manufacturing, and so on, found that its choice of segment classifications passively dictated what skills it looked for in the employees it hired, what processes it executed, and what actions it took. When staffing, for example, Nortel generally recruited individuals to represent the vertical segments and therefore ended up with employees who had a vertical-segment perspective, focus, and mentality. Sales teams, marketing campaigns, and communication programs were devised for these segments. Engineers and designers thought about the markets from a vertical-segment perspective and attempted to fine-tune product offerings to meet segment-specific needs, guided by managers who might decide, for instance, that a particular feature should be added to a product because that feature appealed to a vertical segment in which the company needed to gain market share. In effect, Nortel's market and product strategy, resource selection, and capabilities were being dictated by a vertical-segment classification it had initially chosen for sales, marketing, and accounting purposes. This misapplication of segment classification data is common in many firms because traditional segmentation schemes create convenient targets for strategists and developers, but those targets are seldom worth hitting when it comes to innovation.

It is important to note that applying outcome-based segmentation does *not* force a company to change the way it collects and tracks sales and accounting data. An outcome-based segmentation scheme can operate independently (helping companies communicate to customers), create new products and services, and define the customer value proposition, regardless of how sales and financial results are tracked.

Why Are Traditional Segmentation Methods Ineffective for Purposes of Innovation?

When it comes to using segmentation to help with new product and service creation, many companies simply adopt a convenient classification scheme and impose it on customers with the hope and expectation that customers will act according to the dictates of the categories the scheme outlines. Using this logic, companies may, for example, segment their markets into small, medium, and large businesses and expect that all their customers in the small-business segment will have a set of requirements that they share with each other but not with customers in the medium-size- and large-size-business segments. Similarly, they will expect all their customers in the medium-size-business segment to have a set of requirements shared only by other medium-size businesses and not by small or large businesses, and so on. The hope is that each segment of users represents a homogeneous, nonoverlapping population that reacts predictably and in unison to new products and services.

Unfortunately, that hope is simply not justified when companies use traditional segmentation methods. Traditional segmentation schemes often lead companies to focus on phantom targets—that is, groups of customers who are neither homogeneous nor nonoverlapping, and who may not value a unique set of desired outcomes. These arbitrary classifications fail to honor our basic tenets of solid segmentation theory, which state that an effective segmentation scheme must create a population that:

- Has a unique set of underserved or overserved outcomes
- Represents a sizable portion of the population
- Is homogeneous—meaning that the population agrees on which outcomes are underserved or overserved and responds in the same manner to appropriately targeted products and services
- Makes an attractive strategic target—one that fits with the philosophy and competencies of the firm
- Can be reached through marketing and sales efforts

Although managers know they are trying to find groups of customers with unique requirements who will value a unique set of product or service features, they just can't seem to identify those groups in a predictable and reliable manner. One reason for this goes back to the way companies define "requirement." If a company defines a requirement as a solution, specification, need, or benefit, as examined in Chapter 2, then it is using the wrong customer inputs as the bases for segmenting the market. Needs-based segmentation came close to getting it right, but there is no common agreement as to just what a "need" is. In the needs-based studies we have examined in the past, we found that the segmentation variables included what we would describe as solutions, specifications, needs, benefits, and the occasional outcome. With such a variety of statements being used as inputs, it is no wonder that needs-based segmentation by and large fails to predictably and reliably address the key innovation challenges of development and marketing. Clearly, the key to successful segmentation lies in finding unique segments of opportunity, that is, groups of customers with unique sets of underserved outcomes. The only way to discover those segments is to use outcomes as the basis for segmentation.

What Is Different About Outcome-Based Segmentation?

As we have established, customers buy products and services to help them get jobs done, and their desired outcomes are the metrics they use to describe just what it will take to get the job done perfectly. Desired outcomes that are underserved represent opportunities for improvement. But not everybody in a market agrees on which outcomes are underserved, and as a result in most markets there exists different groups of customers who want to see improvements made along different dimensions. Among those who use circular saws, for example, some may evaluate all the outcomes relating to speed as important and unsatisfied because they can't wait to get through a job, while another group may evaluate all the outcomes associated with making a perfect cut as important and unsatisfied because they are perfectionists who take great pride in their work.

Outcome-based segmentation methods make it possible for companies to define segments such as these. This is only possible because the approach incorporates two distinctive practices: it uses the customers' desired outcomes as the bases for segmenting the market, and, most importantly, the numerical value around which the clustering is executed is not the importance value, but the opportunity score for that outcome. This point is critical. Using the opportunity score as the segmentation variable forces the creation of segments that represent unique opportunities. From a development and marketing perspective this is nirvana, as this market insight is just what is needed to make effective targeting, positioning, messaging, and other product and marketing decisions.

The food and agribusiness conglomerate J. R. Simplot Company used this approach to discover a segment of restaurateurs who wanted a french fry that would last longer in holding without losing its attractive properties. This outcome was not considered underserved by other segments of the market. The dental-products company Dentsply discovered a segment of dentists that feel that the quality of a restoration depends on their ability to consistently and predictably produce solid bonds—a set of outcomes that other segments did not consider underserved. Bosch discovered a segment of drill-driver users who wanted the tool optimized for driving and rarely used it as a drill, unlike other segments of users. Companies trying to identify segments, such as these, must use outcomes and opportunity scores as the basis for market segmentation.

How Is Outcome-Based Segmentation Performed?

To examine the outcome-driven methodology in detail, let's consider as an example Motorola's Radio Products Group, which manufactures mobile radios that are installed in vehicles and used to communicate with a dispatcher, a central location, or other two-way radio users. In 1997, after experiencing limited growth in what appeared to be a maturing market, Motorola was looking for new ways to achieve its growth objectives.

For years, Motorola had been using a vertical industry classification system to segment the radio market, although it recognized the inconsistencies in customer behavior within and across the resulting segments. Intuitively, the company knew another segmentation structure existed, but managers were unable to define it. They opted to pursue outcome-driven segmentation using the following four-step methodology:

1. Collect the required data
2. Choose the segmentation criteria

3. Conduct cluster analysis
4. Profile the clusters

The result was the discovery of useful segments of opportunity.

Collecting the Required Data

The data required to create outcome-based segments is, logically, customers' desired outcomes. Motorola found, for example, that radio users had nearly 100 desired outcomes when using radio products. For example, they wanted to minimize the number of communications that were intercepted by unauthorized parties, to minimize the likelihood of inadvertently making changes to the settings, and to minimize the number of communications that are misunderstood. Having captured those outcomes, Motorola designed a survey instrument and administered it to a large number of radio users that comprised an accurate random sample of the user population. The survey was designed to capture and quantify the importance that users placed on each outcome and the degree to which they felt that each outcome was satisfied by the products currently available. As explained in Chapter 3, both data points are needed so opportunity scores can be calculated for each outcome.

Choosing the Segmentation Criteria

Motorola did not use all 100 outcomes to generate the segmentation scheme. To identify those outcomes that would make the best segmentation variables, Motorola first used factor analysis (a common statistical technique) to group like outcomes together into eighteen distinct opportunity-based factors. Next, they chose one outcome from each of those factors that showed the most variation in market response. In factors for which there was no substantial

Table 4.1 Selecting Segmentation Attributes

Segmentation Attributes for Radio Products

1. Minimize the number of messages that are misunderstood
2. Minimize the number of interruptions during a communication
3. Minimize the amount of interference encountered when communicating
4. Minimize the effort required to communicate discreetly
5. Minimize the number of annoying incoming communications
6. Minimize the time it takes to confirm receipt of a communication
7. Minimize the effort required to establish a record of the communication
8. Minimize the number of communications that can be intercepted
9. Minimize the likelihood of making inadvertent changes to established settings
10. Minimize the effort required to program the device
11. Minimize the effort to operate the device with gloves on

variation in market response, no outcomes were chosen. In total, eleven outcomes were selected as segmentation attributes, as shown in Table 4.1.

Conducting Cluster Analysis

Motorola used nonhierarchical clustering algorithms found in commonly used computer-based statistical analysis programs to execute the clustering process. The clustering algorithm focused on the opportunity ratings given to the eleven selected outcomes and placed the respondents surveyed into a predetermined number of segments based on their responses. Motorola decided on a three-segment solution, and the resultant segments contained 40 percent, 28 percent, and 30 percent of the respondents respectively. The clustering algorithm isolated one group of users (segment 1) that rated outcomes 4, 7, and 8 as both important and unsatisfied. The second group it isolated (segment 2) rated outcomes 1, 2, 3, 9, and

Table 4.2 Segment Differences

Segment 1 Opportunities	Segment 2 Opportunities	Segment 3 Opportunities
4. Minimize the effort required to communicate discreetly	1. Minimize the number of messages that are misunderstood	5. Minimize the number of annoying incoming communications
7. Minimize the effort required to establish a record of the communication	2. Minimize the number of interruptions during a communication	6. Minimize the time it takes to confirm receipt of a communication
8. Minimize the number of communications that can be intercepted	3. Minimize the amount of interference encountered when communicating	10. Minimize the effort required to program the device
	9. Minimize the likelihood of making inadvertent changes to established settings	
	11. Minimize the effort to operate the device with gloves on	

11 as important and unsatisfied, while the third group (segment 3) rated outcomes 5, 6, and 10 as important and unsatisfied. The outcomes and opportunities that were unique to each segment are shown in Table 4.2.

Profiling the Clusters

To understand the demographic and psychographic characteristics of the three segments, Motorola began profiling them. The initial survey, in addition to containing the outcome-related questions, contained more than a dozen questions designed to help Motorola understand what characteristics each segment possessed. The questions elicited the users' ages, their job titles, how they used the product and what they used it for, industry classifications, frequency of radio use, geographic location, and several other important descriptors.

These types of questions are instrumental in understanding segment content once the clusters have been created. After analyzing the data, Motorola quickly concluded, for example, that segment 1 "hired" mobile radio products to communicate privately, discreetly, or covertly, without being noticed by others and without being overheard. Members of this segment, who conducted covert operations from inside a vehicle, valued privacy and security-related outcomes. They included federal and state police, security personnel, and similar individuals; were younger users; and were likely found in urban areas. Segment 2, Motorola concluded, "hired" mobile radio products to provide clear, unambiguous, and uninterrupted communications when faced with dangerous, even life-threatening, situations. Members of this segment consisted mainly of firefighters, police, and security personnel that often leave their vehicles to perform assignments but must maintain vehicle contact at all times. Segment 3 "hired" mobile radio products to communicate with teams and groups, to coordinate activities, and to perform administrative tasks. Members of this segment included coast guard personnel, locomotive engineers, and others who make constant use of radio communications throughout the day to carry out their jobs. In contrast to the other segments, members of this segment required neither privacy nor emergency-situation capabilities.

Until this point in 1997, no mobile radio products produced by Motorola or its competitors had addressed the outcomes uniquely desired in each segment with well-matched product and service offerings. There was a one-size-fits-all mentality in the industry. With the discovery of these segments, Motorola was able to optimize a mobile radio product for each segment. The products included new features that addressed previously underserved outcomes and eliminated product features that addressed outcomes of little or no importance to the segment population.

The end result? Better products at a lower price with increased customer satisfaction. The new products accelerated revenue growth to 18 percent in a stagnant market and secured the company's leadership position in mobile radio products.

How Does Outcome-Based Segmentation Address Development and Marketing Challenges?

Innovation, development, and marketing functions encounter six common challenges which can only be addressed through an effective segmentation methodology. Our outcome-driven segment methodology addresses each of these challenges:

- Identifying unique opportunities in mature markets
- Identifying demanding customer segments that may be willing to pay more for more elaborate solutions
- Identifying customer segments that are unattractive and should not be targeted
- Discovering overserved market segments that make attractive entry points for disruptive innovation
- Determining the best way to enter an existing market as a new entrant
- Discovering segments of high potential growth

Identifying Unique Opportunities in Mature Markets

In mature markets companies find it more difficult to discover unique opportunities, and as a result they often begin to compete on price, eroding company profits, and moving the industry toward commoditization. One way to prevail over this dynamic is to find one or more segments of users that are underserved and devise products and services that address the unique opportunities their underserved outcomes represent.

This was Motorola's goal when it applied outcome-driven segmentation to enhance its position in the mobile-radio-products market. Having discovered the three segments of opportunity described earlier, the product team devised unique products for each segment.

For segment 1 (those who wanted privacy), they created a product that included enhanced encryption, a mechanism to prevent others from overhearing a communication, and noiseless operation. For segment 2 (those involved in life-threatening situations), they added voice command technology and emergency locators and modified the interface to accommodate users wearing gloves. For segment 3 (those involved in managing work assignments), they added features that made it easier to program the radio and ensure messages were received. Table 4.3 highlights the distinctions between the three segments and shows the feature set devised to address the opportunities in each segment.

Creating such products makes it possible to compete along new dimensions of value rather than price. By appealing to unique underserved outcomes in specialized segments, companies can

Table 4.3 Segment Distinctions

	Segment 1: Privacy	Segment 2: Emergency	Segment 3: Administrative
Outcomes Desired	• Discreet communications • Record of communications • Low interceptions	• Clear messages • Few interruptions • Lower interference • Low risk of inadvertent changes to settings • Easy to use with gloves on	• Few unimportant incoming calls • Quick receipt confirmation • Easy to program device
Characteristics	• Covert operations inside vehicle • Younger • High urban concentration	• Firefighters, police, security personnel • Often have to leave vehicle • Must maintain contact at all times	• Coast guard, locomotive engineers, etc • Rely on radio for their daily job • Perform admin tasks
Resulting Solution	• Enhanced encryption • A mechanism to prevent others from overhearing communications • Noiseless operation	• Voice command technology • Emergency locators • Modifications to permit use with gloves	• Easier-to-program radio • Mechanisms to ensure message receipt

devise products that deliver more value, enabling new pricing and positioning strategies. Without this knowledge the trend toward commoditization is likely to continue.

Identifying Demanding Customer Segments That May Be Willing to Pay More for More Elaborate Solutions

In most markets there exists a group of customers who are more demanding than the rest. They are underserved along many dimensions of value; they want more and are willing to pay for it. This segment may be less than 5 percent of the total market or it may be 20 percent or greater. A company benefits from knowing if this segment exists and how large it is.

When Bosch segmented the market for circular saws, they discovered such a segment and targeted the CS20 saw at this segment. This saw included nearly a dozen new product features, all addressing outcomes that were underserved in the most demanding segment of the market. The goal in this case, however, was not to charge a premium price but to increase market share by offering this breakthrough product at a price point that was competitive with other offerings. In December 2004, with nine months of sales data behind it, Bosch was more than realizing its business and growth objectives.

Identifying Customer Segments That Are Unattractive and Should Not Be Targeted

In most markets there also exists a group of customers that is unattractive to target. These customers may be unable to utilize more function, or they may require excessive service while demanding lower prices. Once again, companies benefit from knowing if such a segment exists and how large it is.

When a major insurance provider was looking to expand its customer base, it struggled to find opportunities in the broad market. After completing an outcome-based segmentation analysis, it discovered that a significant percentage of its customers were well satisfied with existing offerings and were unable to utilize more functional value. These customers were only interested in lower prices. By wisely declining to target this segment and instead focusing on the remaining segments, the company discovered a number of solid opportunities that had been masked when it looked at the market as a whole.

Discovering Overserved Market Segments That Make Attractive Entry Points for Disruptive Innovation

A technology can successfully disrupt a market only if a sizable segment of the market population is overserved and willing to accept a product or service that is functionally inferior to those currently available. A disruptive technology often enters the market in a nonthreatening manner, gaining little initial acceptance and outright rejection in most segments because of its poorer performance. As the technology improves, however, it begins to satisfy the outcomes that are important to the mainstream better than the older technologies and so gains acceptance in a larger population—disrupting the market as a whole. When considering a disruptive strategy, managers must be able to determine if overserved segments exist, what their sizes are, and if they make attractive market entry points for disruptive technologies. With this knowledge, a company can confidently define a target segment for disruption—or can be forewarned of its own susceptibility to disruption by others.

In the market for blood glucose monitoring devices, for example, Cygnus, the maker of GlucoWatch is well positioned to address the overserved segment of customers who do not necessarily need more accurate and faster readings, but simply want to know if they are heading off in the wrong direction so they can avoid suffering from a diabetic episode. Accuracy, speed, and other outcomes are less important to this segment, which is willing to accept a product that is inferior along those measures of value so they can get what they need. Over time Cygnus may improve this technology to address the traditional measures of value, and at a lower price point, making it a more attractive product in the mainstream market. This is a good strategy for disruptive innovation.

Determining the Best Way to Enter an Existing Market as a New Entrant

As a new entrant into an existing market, a company must be able to pick out a small segment of customers, address their unique outcomes, and then leverage its position to make gains in other market segments. But what segment makes the best entry point? The ideal segment will likely be small, filled with opportunity, and ignored by the current set of competitors.

Such segments are easily identified using outcome-based segmentation, and these smaller segments are often ignored by established players in the industry because those companies are looking for opportunities that span one or more larger segments of the population. It is difficult to beat established companies at their own game, so using outcome-based segmentation to determine if an attractive entry point exists is even more critical in this situation.

Discovering Segments of High Potential Growth

Companies often ask, "How can a segment of high potential growth be identified and sized before it emerges?" Companies often rely on financial data to determine a segment's size in terms of the revenue it has generated in the past. It is impossible to use this approach to size segments for which products have yet to be developed, however, as they have yet to generate revenue. Outcome-based segmentation solves this problem by identifying and sizing a segment from a nonfinancial perspective.

Take the day-trader segment in the securities market, for example, which was created and led by E*Trade. From a traditional market measurement and segmentation perspective, the day-trader market showed little revenue or growth potential in the early 1990s. At the time, traders who wanted to make many transactions within short periods of time could only do so by holding a seat on the Board of Exchange. With a limited number of seats—and a seat price that exceeded the annual incomes of most people—it is not surprising that this segment appeared relatively small from a revenue-producing perspective. As a result, companies were discouraged from making investments in it.

However, if companies such as Merrill Lynch had studied the market from an outcome-driven perspective, they would have seen a very different picture. They would have found that a good number of people who wanted to make trades wanted to increase the number of trades that could be made per day, minimize the time it took to complete a trade, and minimize the cost of making a trade—and had little need for support and service. Using outcome-based segmentation, managers would have had a very accurate estimate of how many people found those outcomes to be both important and unsatisfied. The percentage of people in this segment and the size of the market would then have been defined. The reality is, the segment already existed; people were simply waiting for a solution that would satisfy their underserved outcomes and make day trading feasible. When that solution appeared, people were quick to act, generating revenues for companies such as E*Trade and thus establishing the day-trader market from a traditional, financial perspective.

How Is Job-Based Segmentation Different, and When Should It Be Used?

Throughout this chapter we have discussed outcome-based segmentation, but when companies are trying to discover new markets to pursue, they often turn to job-based segmentation. How do the two types of segmentation differ? Outcome-based segmentation is used to discover segments of opportunity in a specific market of interest. Job-based segmentation is used to discover entirely new markets—a job or a group of jobs that are underserved. The steps taken to execute each segmentation method are exactly the same with one exception: job-based segmentation uses jobs, not outcomes, as the basis for segmentation.

So how do companies find new markets of interest? Individuals and businesses perform a variety of jobs on a daily basis. The question arises, "What jobs are people trying to get done today that they are unable to get done satisfactorily given the products and services that are currently available?" When a company identifies a job or a group of jobs that are underserved, they may have discovered a new market that is worthy of pursuit.

When Microsoft, for example, recently wanted to figure out what other software, hardware, and service-related markets to pursue, it canvased PC users to uncover all the jobs they were trying to get done. Then, through quantitative research, Microsoft determined which jobs were important and underserved. Those with high opportunity scores were potentially attractive market opportunities. Once the company decided which of those markets to pursue, it obtained the customers' desired outcomes for each job of interest in a second round of research. It then determined which outcomes were important and unsatisfied, so it knew precisely where people were struggling when trying to get the job done. Through this combination of research efforts it uncovered new markets and the underserved outcomes in each—and a road map for innovation and growth.

Summary

To address many development and marketing challenges, companies are dependent on segmentation: identifying groups of customers in the market that represent opportunities for innovation and growth. At the center of debate, however, is just what criteria managers should use to define segments that are truly homogeneous. Demographic classifications are commonly used to define customer segments, but as Daniel Yankelovich stated more than forty years ago, "We should discard the old, unquestioned assumption that demographics is always the best way to segment markets."[1]

It is rare even today that a company employs a segmentation scheme that satisfies the basic tenets of solid segmentation theory, that is, a scheme that reveals segments that are filled with opportunity, homogenous in membership, predictable in behavior, different from one another, and reachable through marketing and sales efforts. There are two explanations for this widespread lack of effective segmentation. First, many managers are used to segmenting customers for other purposes, such as tracking and advertising, and for those purposes attribute-based categories such as product type, price point, age, business size, and so on are relevant and useful. Second, many companies have been unable to develop an effective method of identifying truly homogenous groups of customers with optimal innovation potential. As a result, they have fallen back on familiar segmentation schemes, even though those schemes are inappropriate or downright harmful for innovation efforts.

Outcome-based segmentation is different. It has been optimized to address the innovation challenges faced by development and marketing. It honors the basic tenets of sound segmentation theory and uncovers segments of opportunity. Outcome-based segmentation

---

1. Daniel Yankelovich, "New Criteria for Market Segmentation," *Harvard Business Review* (March–April 1964), 89.

uses the customer's desired outcomes as the bases for segmentation, and it uses the opportunity score for each outcome as the variable for segment creation.

With the ability to identify underserved and overserved segments in a market and the ability to size each segment, companies are able to address many of the key development and marketing challenges that arise when executing innovation and growth strategies. With outcome-based segmentation, strategists and marketing managers no longer inadvertently target phantom segments; instead, their efforts focus on segments of opportunity, and the results are growth, cost reduction, and successful strategies for disruptive innovation.

Targeting Opportunities for Growth

Deciding Where to Focus the Value Creation Effort

- *What is different about targeting for innovation?*
- *What types of broad-market opportunities are likely to be attractive?*
- *What segment-specific targeting strategies are effective?*
- *How does a targeting strategy result in a unique and valued competitive position?*
- *Why do companies fail to target key opportunities?*

The first four steps in the outcome-driven innovation process are aimed at uncovering all of the opportunities that exist in a market, whether they are broad-market opportunities or unique segments of opportunity. If a company does not know with certainty where the market is underserved and overserved, it is more likely to make the wrong investments in new product and service development. It is also more likely to hesitate to take any action at all because it lacks the confidence needed to move forward with conviction. But once a company knows all the opportunities that exist in a market, it can devise a very effective targeting strategy; one that will ultimately place it in a unique and valued competitive position— a position that addresses the underserved outcomes in a market while reducing costs in those areas that are overserved. This is the fifth step in the outcome-driven innovation process. This chapter describes how companies can target the best opportunities for growth and achieve a competitive position that is both unique and valued. It is with these skills that a company translates research into a strategy for successful innovation.

What Is Different About Targeting for Innovation?

Targeting, as defined here, is the process of selecting for pursuit those underserved and overserved outcomes that represent the best opportunities for growth and innovation. This definition of targeting contrasts with the traditional definition, which typically refers to targeting as the process of selecting a market or a segment of customers to pursue. In this stage of the outcome-driven method, we are not concerned with targeting customers; we are focused on targeting the opportunities that overserved or underserved outcomes represent.

An effective targeting strategy requires that a company select— with surgical precision—the opportunities that it will pursue. An effective targeting strategy will enable a company to add function and performance (but not necessarily cost) in areas that are underserved and to reduce cost and function in areas that are overserved. Product and service offerings must deliver all the performance that can be absorbed *but no more*, so that customers are not paying for function they do not need. That is, companies must find that fine balance between delivering too much and too little function.

When targeting opportunities for growth, we suggest that companies target broad-market opportunities first and then target the segment-specific opportunities, handpicking those to pursue over time. As described in Chapters 3 and 4, when searching for opportunities, we first look across the broad market, which is defined as the entire customer population. When targeting opportunities, the approach is no different. It is best to target a big opportunity in the broad market first because an innovation that has broad-market appeal will have a big impact on revenue growth. Once the opportunities in the broad market are addressed or exhausted, the segment-specific opportunities should be explored and considered given their size, business implications, and potential impact on revenue growth.

What Types of Broad-Market Opportunities Are Likely to Be Attractive?

When considering the broad market, companies should look for the types of opportunities that are known to result in breakthrough products and/or increased market share. Our experiences have led us to identify five types of broad-market opportunities, each of which represents a unique avenue for growth and innovation:

- Related opportunities that form a theme
- Unrelated opportunities that represent growth avenues
- A single opportunity that can be addressed with a new, ancillary product
- Overserved outcomes that add unnecessarily to product cost
- Opportunities for technology development and long-term growth

Related Opportunities That Form a Theme

On occasion we find a market in which a number of underserved outcomes—which is to say, a number of opportunities—represent some sort of theme. In such a case a company is advised to message, position, and compete around this theme, as it offers a strong competitive position. Consider, for example, the U.S.-based skin- and wound-care division of Coloplast, the Danish medical device company, which applied outcome-driven thinking to improve its revenue and market share position. Competitors in that market traditionally positioned their products and services around making wounds better and adopted faster healing time as a common positioning theme. Coloplast discovered, however, that eight of the top twelve opportunities in the market were not at all related to helping to make the wound better—they were related to actions that would inadvertently make the wound worse. They found that wound-care nurses wanted to minimize the length of time the patient's skin is wet or moist from urine, perspiration, and stool; increase the patient's systemic ability to heal; minimize the likelihood of a skin irritation getting worse; minimize the rate of fungal or bacterial growth on the skin; and minimize the likelihood of a healed wound breaking down again.

Coloplast targeted these related outcomes even though moving away from the theme of faster healing time was counterintuitive. But the opportunities were clear, and pursuing them proved very profitable. Coloplast called its new theme "preventing complications" and adopted this theme in its positioning, pipeline prioritization, and new product development activities. David Hotchkiss, the vice president of sales and marketing for Coloplast, told us recently that the outcome-driven perspective was instrumental in helping the company identify a unique and marketable position for their skin- and wound-care business. By adopting the "preventing complications" theme as part of their positioning strategy, they were able to achieve double-digit growth within six months in a fairly mature market. Understanding which outcomes represented the best opportunities for improvement gave them a huge advantage over their competition.

Broad-market opportunity themes such as this typically offer the best chance for growth and innovation. When all customers agree that the outcomes are important and no competitor has yet addressed them, then the company that first seizes on the theme will enjoy a strategic coup.

Unrelated Opportunities That Represent Growth Avenues

If the market does not contain a group of opportunities that form a specific theme, companies should not lose hope. Unrelated opportunities can also represent attractive growth avenues, provided their opportunity scores are high enough. When Bosch, for example, applied the outcome-driven approach to its circular saw market, they discovered ten opportunities in a market that has been around for about eighty years. These opportunities were not related or tied to a theme, but by addressing the underserved outcome that each opportunity represented, Bosch was able to create a winning product in a crowded field. The innovative Bosch CS20 circular saw resulted not from a breakthrough in any one area, but from solid improvements in all the remaining areas of opportunity such as minimizing downtime when the cord is cut and minimizing the likelihood of the cut veering off the cut path. The chances of identifying those areas of opportunity and having the confidence to create a new product around them without using the outcome-driven approach are slim, and that is why the Bosch CS20's combination of features had never been included in any earlier saw.

A Single Opportunity That Can Be Addressed with a New, Ancillary Product

Even when there are not a large number of opportunities in the broad market, there may be one big opportunity that has not yet been addressed. A big opportunity is defined here as an underserved outcome that has an opportunity score greater than 15. Such an opportunity is crying out for a company to take advantage of it with an innovative solution. Big opportunities are uncommon in most industries and usually exist only because of technology constraints, but there may be a way to address them. The trick is to pursue the big opportunity not with an improved product feature, but with a new product that assists the existing product in getting a job done.

Take Cordis Corporation, the medical device company mentioned earlier. Back in 1993–1994 when it applied outcome-driven thinking to the angioplasty balloon market, they found that among the eighty or so desired outcomes of interventional cardiologists who perform the angioplasty procedure, minimizing the likelihood that the treated blood vessel would become narrowed once again after treatment represented the biggest opportunity for improvement, with an opportunity score above 15. Rather than adding a feature to the angioplasty balloon to help address the outcome, they created an entirely new product—the stent—that was packaged and sold separately. It became the fastest-selling medical device in history and created a $1 billion industry in less than two years.

The targeting principle derived from this situation has been used by other firms to achieve successful results. When a big opportunity is discovered, evaluate whether or not the outcome can be addressed by creating a new product that fits well within the existing system and makes great improvements in getting the job done. Whereas incremental improvements to an existing system would get priced along with the system, a new, ancillary product can be sold separately and at a higher margin, thus creating a new and profitable market.

Overserved Outcomes That Add Unnecessarily to Product Cost

We sometimes find markets or market segments that contain few if any underserved outcomes. This is more common in mature markets or if the product is simple in its function—meaning that it addresses only a small number of obvious outcomes. Cotton swabs

(Unilevers' Q-tips is the well-known brand) and the pen are examples of the latter. With products such as these we often find that the market is overserved, and we determine which overserved outcomes are contributing most to product cost. We then select those outcomes as potential opportunities for cost reduction. Done correctly, a company is able to decrease product performance and reduce product cost without reducing customer satisfaction to the point that it creates an opportunity for improvement. This balancing act may be difficult to achieve, but it is nearly impossible to achieve when the most costly overserved outcomes are unknown.

Many software applications suffer from the problem of overserving the outcomes for which they were originally designed. In the software industry, however, the overserved outcomes rarely get addressed because the unneeded function does not add to the cost of the product. Because software is unique, companies in this industry need to consider whether or not the unneeded function is negatively impacting the user's ability to get a job done. If it is, the developer may be able to charge more for a simpler version of the same application.

Opportunities for Technology Development and Long-Term Growth

The types of opportunities discussed thus far lend themselves to short-term action. But not all opportunities can be addressed in the next release of a product. Some underserved outcomes will require new technology, cost-reduced technology, or a reshaped technology before the outcomes are effectively pursued. These opportunities become good long-term targets that can be explored by a company's research and development function.

When Motorola's R&D team, for example, discovered several years ago that eleven underserved outcomes in the market for mobile radios could potentially be addressed by voice command technology, they changed their strategy. Prior to the research they had pursued a technology development plan that only addressed four of the eleven outcomes. Knowing about the other seven related outcomes made it possible to develop the technology along other important dimensions, shaping it to increase the overall value that was delivered.

What Segment-Specific Targeting Strategies Are Effective?

Once the broad-market opportunities have been tackled, the only worthwhile remaining growth options may be hidden within the outcome-based segments. Finding and targeting such opportunities can present some unique challenges as certain tactics may work well in one situation but not in others. We have devised four segment-specific targeting strategies and rules that have proven effective over the years:

- Identify opportunities that span multiple outcome-based segments
- Build a single platform for multiple segment-specific solutions
- Pursue the least-challenging segments of opportunity first
- Target segments that represent attractive price points

Identify Opportunities That Span Multiple Outcome-Based Segments

When a broad-market opportunity does not exist, companies often look for opportunities that multiple segments share. This makes sense: even if there isn't an opportunity to address underserved outcomes for 100 percent of the population, there may be one that will address 50 or 60 percent of the population, making it an attractive opportunity to pursue. Such opportunities are typically discovered by analyzing the market segments with underserved outcomes and determining which opportunities, if any, are common across them.

A major insurance company, for example, found no big opportunities across the auto insurance market, but did find that all the
underserved segments wanted to minimize the likelihood that new
customers were being given better rates and minimize the time it
took to compare different firms' rates, along with a number of other
outcomes. By addressing these opportunities they were able to add
value for over 50 percent of the market population.

Build a Single Platform for Multiple Segment-Specific Solutions

When a company is able to find opportunities that are shared by
multiple segments, it may be able to define a feature set that
addresses those shared opportunities and use that feature set as a
platform on which to build solutions for the multiple segments,
thereby reducing the overall number of product platforms that it
needs. This thinking is shown in Figure 5.1: a single set of features
is created to address the common opportunities, and unique feature
sets are added to that platform to satisfy the remaining underserved
outcomes in the three targeted segments.

Motorola's Radio Products Group, for example, used this thinking to limit the number of technology platforms it needed to develop
a full line of mobile radios. Platform development and support typically cost tens of millions of dollars over the life of a product, so

Figure 5.1 Build a Platform for Segment-Specific Solutions

Segment 1 Opportunities and Features	Segment 2 Opportunities and Features	Segment 3 Opportunities and Features

Common Opportunities, Common Features

Create a product platform that addresses the common segment opportunities and develop
segment-specific solutions that pursue the unique opportunities in each segment.

reducing the number of platforms a company needs is a solid, cost-reduction strategy.

Pursue the Least-Challenging Segments of Opportunity First

When performing outcome-based segmentation, we typically find a segment of the population that is highly underserved—meaning many of their outcomes have high opportunity scores. While at first blush it might seem that this would be the best segment to target, it is rarely the case. This type of segment is typically underserved along so many dimensions that it would be impossible to address all or even most of its underserved outcomes in the next release of the product, and, consequently, it would be impossible to achieve total customer satisfaction with that release. Therefore it's wiser not to target such a segment until all the other attractive segments have been pursued.

When AIG used outcome-based segmentation to segment their agents, for example, they found one very demanding segment (segment 3) and two other underserved but less demanding segments. AIG targeted the least-demanding segment first (segment 1) because they were able to satisfy all the underserved outcomes in that segment with only a handful of new service features. Along the way, those same features helped AIG make some progress in addressing the underserved outcomes in segment 3.

Next AIG targeted the other less demanding segment (segment 2). Here again they were able to address all the underserved outcomes in that segment with a handful of new service features. By combining these features with those devised for segment 1, AIG moved closer to addressing all the underserved outcomes in segment 3. Finally, they added the additional features needed to satisfy the remaining underserved outcomes in segment 3.

This targeting approach, which is often executed over a period of years, has proven to be the most efficient method for increasing market share while systematically working toward addressing the most demanding segment of customers. Taking the opposite approach and going after the most demanding segment first *does not* guarantee that the other underserved segments will be addressed along the way, *and* it requires a significant investment in resource with little short-term benefit.

Target Segments That Represent Attractive Price Points

Occasionally we find a segment that has no or only a small number of underserved outcomes while the remaining segments demand more performance and have greater numbers of underserved outcomes.

In such a situation we may plot the segments with price point along one axis and performance along the other, as shown in Figure 5.2. Such an exercise enables a firm to determine which segment is most likely to be satisfied at a low price point and which will only be satisfied with more features at a higher price point. New market entrants and companies that are looking to disrupt the market will

Figure 5.2 Targeting Around Price Points

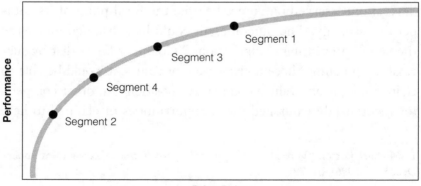

find that targeting the lowest price-point segment first is often the best strategy. This strategy works because by targeting the least-demanding segment or an overserved segment, a company has the best chance of delivering all the needed value while operating within a profitable business model that existing competitors are unlikely to be able to copy.

How Does a Targeting Strategy Result in a Unique and Valued Competitive Position?

At the heart of competition and strategy, according to Harvard Business School professor Michael Porter, is the ability to define a competitive position that is unique and valued by customers.[1] Outcome-driven studies and the opportunities they identify provide the information that companies need to define such a competitive position systematically.

Keep in mind just how we define an opportunity—it is an outcome that is important to the customer and not well satisfied by the product and service solutions that are currently available. This means that no one has been able to successfully satisfy that outcome. The first company to do so will separate itself from the pack and earn a unique competitive position.

Take the example of Coloplast's skin- and wound-care division. Several underserved outcomes became the focal point of its competitive strategy. The outcomes all could be subsumed under the theme of "preventing complications." Coloplast knew that by successfully pursuing those underserved outcomes, it would be able to claim a unique and valued competitive position. No other competitor recognized or pursued those opportunities or claimed to help

---

1. Michael Porter, "What Is Strategy?" *Harvard Business Review* (November–December 1996), 61–78.

customers prevent complications, which made Coloplast's position unique. Coloplast's subsequent sales and development efforts specifically addressed the underserved outcomes, and customers responded positively because they valued the improvements.

Companies often struggle to formulate an effective competitive strategy because they do not know which customer outcomes are underserved by their products and those of their competitors. An outcome-driven targeting strategy identifies underserved outcomes and then points to the ones that it will be most advantageous to pursue—the ones that have the potential to secure for the company a competitive position that is both unique and valued. The ability to statistically validate the existence of those opportunities and potential positions brings much-needed discipline to the art of competitive strategy.

Why Do Companies Fail to Target Key Opportunities?

In Chapter 3 we discussed why opportunities often go undiscovered—namely, because companies do not have a clear definition of what an opportunity is, do not get the customer inputs they need to uncover opportunities, and lack effective methods for prioritizing opportunities. We also explained how these issues are overcome so opportunities can be defined, prioritized, and ultimately targeted. What we want to address here is why some companies fail to target the uncovered opportunities even after they have discovered what opportunities exist.

When faced with a set of prioritized opportunities, managers must reconcile the existence of those opportunities with what they already know and believe. Assuming the data are correct, managers have only a couple of options: accept the data and act on it, or reject the data in favor of a competing set of beliefs.

We would argue that acting on the data is the only logical option, but we have on rare occasion worked with managers that have spent the company's time and money gathering outcome-driven information only to refute and ignore the data in the end. Why? Based on our subsequent undercover work in this area, we have found that managers choose to invalidate data when:

They do not get the "right" answer back. We find that managers will sometimes commission research to help them validate an idea they have been backing and want to pursue. If the research fails to validate their hypothesis, they may decide to refute or ignore the data.

They feel the results threaten their jobs. In a couple of situations we have seen mangers refute the results because accepting them would place the managers in a bad light and might result in the loss of their jobs. This is most likely to happen when the research reveals opportunities in areas that others have suspected all along, but that the managers themselves have failed to identify. They naturally want to protect their reputations, but doing so may be at the company's expense.

Addressing the opportunities would require the development of a new competency. We also find that managers will refute the results when accepting them would force the managers to develop new competencies within the organization, and the managers are not interested or are unwilling to take on that added responsibility.

So, how do managers who are intent on ignoring the results go about refuting their validity? We have seen two methods of attack attempted. The first method is simply to attack the data collection methodology (the survey, recruiting methods, sample design), to cast doubt on the validity of the research overall. The second method is to commission other studies, purposely designed to deliver conflicting results, or to use data from other existing studies to try and invalidate the results.

Companies need to know what opportunities exist in a market in order to succeed, and they need to be willing to address those opportunities—regardless of what the opportunities are. There are only so many opportunities in a market. To ignore those that are discovered is certainly not acceptable practice if a firm wants to grow.

Summary

When the opportunities for improvement have been revealed in a market, company managers must decide which ones to pursue. An effective targeting strategy adds function and performance (but not necessarily cost) in areas that are underserved and reduces cost and function in areas that are overserved. A company's product and service offerings must deliver all the performance that can be absorbed *but no more*, so that customers are not paying for function they do not need.

Several types of broad-market opportunities exist:

- Related opportunities that form a theme
- Unrelated opportunities that represent growth avenues
- A single opportunity that can be addressed with a new, ancillary product
- Overserved outcomes that add unnecessarily to product cost
- Opportunities for technology development and long-term growth

Segment-specific opportunities revealed through outcome-based segmentation offer several additional avenues for value creation.

Knowing which opportunities to target for growth has a dramatic impact on all subsequent actions a firm takes. No longer will the firm have to fear failing because it has expended resources on overserved outcomes or improved satisfaction levels for some outcomes at the expense of others. Instead, it will be able to act with the confidence that its investment of resources will result in the solid creation of customer value.

CHAPTER

Positioning Current Products

Connecting Opportunities with Valued Product Features

- *Why does messaging often fail to tout a product's true value?*
- *What are the prerequisites for an effective messaging strategy?*
- *What messaging will be most effective?*
- *Should a company message along an emotional or functional dimension?*
- *How does the sales force have immediate impact on revenue generation?*
- *What is the advantage of an outcome-based brand?*

Once a company has targeted the underserved outcomes that represent the best opportunities for growth and innovation, it is able to exploit those opportunities and gain revenue in three distinct ways:

- By better communicating and exploiting any advantages its current products have in satisfying the targeted underserved outcomes, leading to increased sales

- By quickly bringing to market those products and services in development that do the best job of addressing the targeted opportunities
- By developing longer-term product and service ideas that target the remaining unexploited opportunities

When Cordis Corporation, for example, targeted fifteen underserved outcomes in 1994, it realized that its current angioplasty balloon products already addressed three of those outcomes—the company had just never told anybody. To exploit its advantages, Cordis refined its messaging and sales strategy and publicized the fact that its products addressed those opportunities. The company's market share went from 1 to 5 percent within six months based purely on the new messaging. Next, Cordis looked at its development pipeline and recognized that the stent, which was one of about forty projects in the pipeline, specifically addressed the largest market opportunity—minimizing the likelihood that a treated blood vessel would become narrowed once again. In response, the company reprioritized its development resources, placing more developers on the stent. With the added resources, Cordis was the first manufacturer to bring such a product to market. As mentioned in Chapter 5, the stent turned out to be the fastest-growing medical device in history. But Cordis did not stop there. It devised a new set of product features that addressed the remaining dozen or so underserved outcomes it had identified, and eighteen months later released a line of angioplasty balloon products that took the company from 5 percent to 20 percent market share and made it the market leader in the angioplasty balloon market. These are the kinds of gains that are possible when companies take the next steps in the outcome-driven methodology.

Chapters 7 and 8 address the question of new product development by exploring pipeline prioritization and the creation of breakthrough products, respectively; Chapter 6 shows how companies can improve sales of their current products. This is the sixth step in the outcome-driven innovation process. The approach is straightforward: companies must assess how well their current products address today's opportunities and then augment their positioning, messaging, and branding strategies accordingly. When an existing product or service satisfies one or more underserved outcomes well, the company must communicate that fact to the customer. A solid messaging strategy that informs customers of product advantages typically results in new growth with current products.

Why Does Messaging Often Fail to Tout a Product's True Value?

A company can have a great product, but if it fails to communicate the product's value, it will not optimize its sales revenue. Although marketing managers know this, we have found that positioning and messaging strategies often fail to communicate a product's true value because companies are unaware of the opportunities that exist in a market, use vague messaging that fails to hit the mark, and stick with outdated messages.

Lack of Awareness of the Opportunities That Exist in a Market

As we have established in previous chapters, most companies do not know all the outcomes their customers are trying to achieve or which of those outcomes are underserved. Without that basic knowledge, how can a company expect to devise a messaging and communications strategy that makes a solid connection between a product's features and the customer's underserved outcomes? Without the needed information, it would take a stroke of luck to connect product features with underserved outcomes. Companies that do not know where market opportunities can be found are more likely to message around outcomes that are unimportant or outcomes that are already satisfied and will therefore fail to communicate the product's true potential value. Before completing outcome-based work, one software company, for example, was ready with the messaging for its new product, but it failed to connect the strengths of the product to the underserved outcomes. They would have missed the mark, but they changed the messaging to have the most impact.

Vague Messaging That Fails to Hit the Mark

Companies often use needs-related adjectives such as "reliable," "consistent," and "robust," or benefits-related adjectives such as "faster," "better," and "cheaper," in their communications and messaging. But as we learned in Chapter 2, these types of statements are vague, imprecise, and open to interpretation. They are unlikely to communicate a product's true value.

When a razor manufacturer, for example, makes the claim that its razor, which has a new rubberized handle, is easy to use, customers are left on their own to figure out what makes it easy to use is the fact that the rubberized handle helps minimize the likelihood of dropping the razor when it is wet (an underserved outcome). They may or may not make the connection, and those who fail to do so will not understand the true value of the product and will be less likely to buy it. In general, needs and benefits statements do not pinpoint the advantage one product has over another. The customer must fill in the blanks, which means that success is left to chance. Why run that risk? Precision, not vagueness, is the key to communicating a product's true value.

Outdated Messages

Companies that take an outcome-driven approach to innovation know that although outcome statements are stable over time, once an outcome is satisfied, it no longer represents an opportunity for improvement. Messages that continue to tout a product's value along a well-served dimension will lose their resonance with customers. This means that a company's messaging and communications strategies must change over time in order to remain effective. Being "stronger than dirt" may be a good message when that feature represents a unique advantage, but once everything on the market is "stronger than dirt," the message becomes meaningless. It fails to connect any other advantages the product may have with the remaining underserved outcomes and, therefore, no longer communicates the true value of the product to the customer. Because value migrates, innovation must be dynamic—and so must messaging. Holding on to a message that no longer resonates will only slow sales and growth.

What Are the Prerequisites for an Effective Messaging Strategy?

It is not only possible but often likely that although a company's current products and services are addressing one or more underserved outcomes, their messaging is not communicating that advantage to the customer. For a messaging strategy to achieve perfect alignment between the company and their customers, several conditions must be met. The company must:

- Be aware of the opportunities that exist—know which outcomes are underserved
- Have a product that truly addresses the underserved outcomes
- Recognize what product features specifically address the underserved outcomes
- Determine if and where the current messaging is off

Breakdowns are common at each step of this process, resulting in faulty positioning and messaging strategies and slow sales.

Be Aware of the Opportunities That Exist

As mentioned earlier, this basic knowledge is a prerequisite to success. Companies must accept that opportunities are defined as underserved and overserved outcomes, have the ability to identify the opportunities in their market, and know how to prioritize and target the identified opportunities. Chapters 1 through 5 show how to achieve those objectives. Once the underserved outcomes are well defined and prioritized, companies can begin the task of formulating an effective messaging and communications strategy.

Have a Product That Truly Addresses the Underserved Outcomes

Once the opportunities are known, a company must determine how well their current products address the underserved outcomes and exploit any unique product strengths. If it is learned, for example, that a company's product outperforms all other competitors in satisfying an outcome that has a high opportunity score, then this reveals a competitive strength in an area that is generally underserved. Letting customers know that a product addresses this underserved outcome will likely result in increased sales. When Coloplast let their customers know that their products helped address several outcomes relating to the prevention of complications, product sales hit double-digit growth levels within six months.

Typically, there are two methods that companies use to see if their products or services address underserved or overserved outcomes. They can either use an external quantitative method that obtains customer satisfaction data directly from customers, or they can use an internal method that requires people within the organization to make an objective assessment of the company's products.

The external method relies on the type of quantitative research activities described in Chapter 3. The results of such an analysis will look like the fictionalized results for the circular saw market shown in Table 3.2 in Chapter 3. In that table, all the competitors had opportunity scores that were relatively close to one another for all the desired outcomes. But suppose Bosch discovered that they performed substantially better than two competitors on one of the outcomes, as shown in Table 6.1 (also presenting fictionalized data). Here, we can see that the biggest opportunity—with an opportunity score of 12.4—is the customer's desire to minimize the time it takes to make bevel adjustments. Although this outcome is generally underserved, 65 percent of the Bosch circular saw users were very satisfied with their ability to achieve this outcome (denoted by the 6.5 in the Bosch column). In contrast, only 38 percent of Makita and 35 percent of DeWalt users were satisfied with their ability to

Table 6.1 How Well Does Your Product Address the Opportunities?

Desired outcomes for a circular saw	Imp	Sat	Opp	Satisfaction			
				Bosch	DeWalt	Makita	Other
Minimize the time it takes to make bevel adjustments	8.3	4.2	12.4	6.5	3.8	3.5	3.3
Minimize the frequency with which the cord gets in the path	8.3	5.3	11.3	5.5	4.6	5.4	4.9
Minimize the percentage of time the cut line is blocked from view	7.6	4.4	10.8	4.6	4.4	4.5	3.2
Minimize the likelihood of debris blowing in the user's eyes	8.5	6.9	10.1	6.5	7.2	7.1	5.9
Minimize the likelihood of snagging the guard on the material	8.7	7.7	9.7	7.8	7.6	7.7	7.3
Minimize the likelihood of getting cut when using the saw	7.6	5.5	9.7	6.2	4.8	5.5	5.5
Minimize the likelihood that the saw will be stolen	6.5	6.1	8.9	6.3	5.9	6.1	5.7
Minimize the likelihood of the cut going off track	6.5	6.2	4.8	6.1	6.3	6.2	6.3
Minimize the frequency of blade change	4.4	6.7	2.1	6.8	6.4	6.7	6.7

achieve this outcome. This suggests that Bosch circular saws are designed in such a way that they do a significantly better job at minimizing the time it takes to make bevel adjustments. It is up to company engineers and management to validate that a strength reported by users is indeed present.

External analysis is preferable to internal analysis because it is inherently objective and relies on actual customer responses. Sometimes, however, it is impossible to obtain a sufficient sample of users for the external method. This may occur when there are few users, the users are unknown, the users are unwilling to admit to using the product, or when the company cannot afford to conduct the research. In those situations, a company must rely on the internal method. The best option is to have an objective team of company employees conduct an introspective evaluation of the company's current products. To ensure that an honest assessment is provided, it is often best to use a cross-functional group whose members are unlikely to have the same outlooks on the products—for example, a team made up of representatives from sales and operations, customer service, engineering, and marketing. Members of the team must be able to evaluate competitive products objectively as well if they are to make a solid comparison and uncover the company's competitive strengths. The data can then be used to draw the needed conclusions.

Recognize What Product Features Specifically Address the Underserved Outcomes

Once a company has determined that it indeed has a competitive strength in an area that is generally underserved, it must be able to determine what it is about its product that is the source of that competitive advantage. If the Bosch circular saw is better at minimizing the time it takes to make bevel adjustments, then the design team must be able to ascertain what it is about the saw that contributes to the delivery of that unique value. Is it the detents on the guide, the quick release mechanism, or some other attribute? Once the answer is discovered, the company will be able to communicate that value to the customer. Rather than telling customers that the saw is easy to use, for example, the company will be able to say that "unique detents enable users to make quick bevel adjustments," solidly connecting a unique product feature to a specific under-served outcome. Making this connection is the key to communicating product value.

Determine If and Where the Current Messaging Is Off

Before devising a new messaging strategy, it is best to evaluate the current strategy and determine exactly where and why the current messaging strategy is ineffective. Such an analysis typically reveals that the messaging strategy is focused on unimportant outcomes, outcomes that are already satisfied or overserved outcomes. One medical device company discovered that most of their messaging (and their advertising budget) was focused on exploiting an outcome that was prioritized sixty-seventh out of ninety outcomes. It was fairly important (7.5), but it was already satisfied (6.5), making it a marginal target for improvement or messaging.

What Messaging Will Be Most Effective?

After a company has determined that a current product does address one or more underserved outcomes successfully, all that is left to do is devise a message that communicates that unique product value to the customer. The company may choose to devise a messaging strategy either around an outcome theme or around a specific outcome.

Create a Message Around a Theme

When a company is lucky enough to find that their product is best at satisfying a number of related underserved outcomes, then they are in a strong position to own that theme. In this case, the best messaging strategy is often devised by aggregating the related outcomes under a higher-level statement that accurately reflects the theme and the underlying outcomes. Coloplast's wound- and skin-care division offers a perfect example. Managers at Coloplast found that their products were perceived as slightly better than others when it came to minimizing the bacteria growth rate in the wound bed, minimizing the amount of necrotic tissue that was present, and for several other outcomes that all related to preventing complications—all of which were important to customers. Coloplast claimed the "preventing complications" theme and communicated this new position to customers. Not surprisingly, the message resonated and sales increased. Discovering and owning this one theme proved invaluable.

Themes are often found by grouping together all the targeted outcomes that are related and giving them a name. It is common for a company to uncover more than one theme when assessing all the targeted outcomes. Syngenta, a seed and crop protection company, for example, found five different themes when they analyzed the 28 outcomes (out of 116) they targeted as representing significant opportunities in the corn-farming market. One theme related to protecting crops from pests and another focused on uniform plant growth. Each of the themes contained three to six outcomes that could stand as positioning and messaging "pillars" over time.

Create a Message Around a Specific Outcome

Companies are more likely to find that their product is better at satisfying just one underserved outcome, rather than several. In this situation it is most effective to make a connection between the feature that is providing that advantage and the specific outcome the feature addresses, as in the example of the Bosch circular saw, for which the message that "unique detents enable users to make quick bevel adjustments" is very effective—short, sweet, and to the point.

Whether the message is created around a theme or a specific outcome, companies are closing the communications gap with customers by focusing customers' attention on the true value of the product.

Should a Company Message Along an Emotional or Functional Dimension?

Thus far we have talked about communicating messages of functionality to customers, but it is also true that customers sometimes have emotional as well as functional jobs that they are trying to get done. When buying a car, for example, the buyer's emotional jobs may include feeling successful, having a sense of self-satisfaction, or being attractive to others, while his or her functional jobs may include transporting passengers, transporting goods, and finding the most direct route to his or her destination.

Companies often feel the need to appeal to their customers' emotions, but depending on the functional and emotional complexity of the product or service being delivered, doing so can bring unexpected and unwanted results. When Motorola's cell phone division, for example, felt Nokia breathing down its neck in 1997, managers knew they had to try something different. They feared that their products were no longer exciting people and recognized that their marketing and messaging campaigns were failing to capture the public's imagination. They brought in marketing experts who had been trained by some of the world's leading marketing companies, including Procter & Gamble and Pepsi. The experts quickly realized that Motorola's products had no emotional appeal and that a makeover was desperately needed.

In response, Motorola introduced a number of cell phone products that were branded with names such as Accompli (for those who want to be on the cutting edge), Vdot (for those who want to feel important), Timeport (for those who want to feel productive), and Talkabout (for those who want to feel in close contact with loved ones). Each brand was intended to appeal to the unique emotional sensibilities of different segments of cell phone buyers. Years later, Motorola found itself abandoning what turned out to be a failed strategy that cost the company time and resources in a fast-moving market and that led to much of the disarray the company continues to experience. What went wrong? What did the marketing experts fail to see?

In the years we have spent analyzing the vagaries of marketing, we have found that certain products—those in the cosmetic and perfume industries—are relatively simple, functionally speaking and are often purchased to help customers get emotional jobs done (such as feeling attractive to others). Products such as these need only satisfy maybe a dozen or so customer outcomes. Perfume need only satisfy outcomes related to scent, strength, bottle shape, and packaging. As the markets for these types of products mature, the products' simplicity makes it difficult for companies to continue to differentiate one product from another along functional dimensions—there are too few from which to choose. This in effect forces manufacturers to differentiate their products along an emotional dimension in order to build and maintain brand loyalty. For these companies, emotion-based messaging skills are necessary for survival.

At the other end of the spectrum we find companies in industries that produce highly functional items such as medical devices, financial services, and computer and software tools—all products that must satisfy 50 to 150 desired outcomes or more. Such products can be differentiated along many functional dimensions, and customers who buy and use such products rarely use them to get emotional jobs done. Interventional cardiologists, for example, who perform angioplasty and stent procedures, are not focused on how a particular brand makes them feel when performing the procedure. They are concerned purely with the product's functional ability to complete the procedure. It would be ridiculous to try to build brand loyalty with interventional cardiologists based only on that type of emotional appeal. Loyalty must be built through the continual delivery of superior function.

It appears, then, that when a company such as Motorola that produces highly functional products tries to take a page from the Procter & Gamble playbook and adopts emotional branding, it is sure to fail. Cell phones are functionally complex, and back in the late 1990s much of that function had yet to be perfected and exploited. Basic functions, such as not dropping a call, for example, still represented a large opportunity for improvement in this market. Only when all or most of the needed function was delivered would it be worth considering differentiation along an emotional dimension.

To summarize our findings, we have categorized the possible scenarios into four quadrants based on their combination of functional and emotional characteristics, as shown in Figure 6.1.

Figure 6.1   Emotion vs. Function

jewelry	
cosmetics	apparel automobiles
food and beverages	
packaged goods **quadrant 2**	**quadrant 3**
	electronics
	appliances
chemicals	software
	services
raw materials	medical devices
quadrant 1	**quadrant 4**

Emotional Complexity

Functional Complexity

In quadrant 1 (low function, low emotion) we find industries involved in the production of raw materials and chemicals. Since products in these industries have very few functional outcomes or emotional jobs associated with them, companies in this quadrant are better off positioning and differentiating their products along another dimension altogether, such as service or cost. Dow Corning, for example, takes this approach with its silicon products. They have a low-cost business model they call Ziameter; if customers want value-added services, they can purchase the same products at a somewhat higher cost under the Dow Corning brand.

In quadrant 2 (low function, high emotion) we find the cosmetics, food and beverage, and packaged-goods industries. These industries spend considerable time differentiating along emotional dimensions—as well they should, since many of these products have limited function. Much is to be gained, however, by trying to make these products more functional. It not only adds a new avenue for differentiation, but it also makes the product more valuable to the user. Functional foods have become a product category in and of themselves. Companies in the beverage industry, such as Red Bull, SoBe, and Glacieu, are "going functional" by adding ingredients that go beyond satisfying thirst. Products that help improve energy levels, physical performance, and concentration enable customers to get more jobs done, which makes the products more valuable from a functional standpoint.

In quadrant 3 (high function, high emotion) we find the apparel and automotive industries. Although products in these industries are highly functional, they are also very important in defining the customer's persona—defining who he or she is in the eyes of other people. Because of this, the emotional component is an important dimension of differentiation. That is not to say, however, that the functional dimension can be overlooked. A well-orchestrated messaging and branding strategy for markets that fall in this quadrant should address both. In the automotive industry we see Lexus successfully addressing both function and emotion with a well-balanced messaging strategy.

In the clothing industry designers often try to appeal to a customer's emotions—this is a critical aspect of most designer brands. But I believe that some name-brand designers (an example would be those whose clothing is an extension of their perfume line) fail to give the functional aspect of clothing enough consideration. Conversely, clothing companies that are focused on function, such as Tommy Bahama and the Gap, have had great success in recent years. To get it right, designers must consider both the functional and emotional dimensions of the product.

In quadrant 4 (high function, low emotion) we find electronics, software, services, and medical-device industries. As stated earlier, the focus here needs to be on function, as these products have little emotional appeal. Here, the challenge is to figure out along which functional dimensions a product should be differentiated. Then too, once a company can successfully address underserved outcomes in the functional realm, it may be able to look for value in the emotional realm without suffering Motorola's fate. Apple Computer is well known for having added an emotional dimension to its computers and media players—but only after making them highly functional.

Getting that balance of functionality and emotion is especially tricky when the jobs the product addresses are ambiguous. Hallmark's party division for example, serves customers who often make purchase decisions along some emotional dimension, such as the desire "to make my child think I am the best parent in the world." But once a parent makes the decision to throw a party for a child, the job of doing so without a hitch becomes purely functional. It would be a mistake for Hallmark to place most of its emphasis on the emotional dimension and ignore the functional component.

So what can we learn from all this? Different markets require different messaging strategies. Motorola made the mistake of thinking that a strategy that worked well for marketing giants would work well for Motorola—without taking into account the fact that those marketing giants were in low-function markets, whereas Motorola is in a high-function market.

Generally speaking, companies should base their messaging strategies on the functional jobs and outcomes their customers are trying to achieve and move toward emotional appeal only after a product's function has been just about fully exploited. An example from the sporting-goods industry provides a good illustration. Some readers may remember back in the 1960s when PF Flyers were the popular sneaker of choice. They addressed just a few of the functional concerns of users, giving some needed support and stabilization. Years later, Converse sneakers became popular as they did a much better job of addressing the user's functional jobs and outcomes. But Converse did not try to appeal to buyers' emotions. It took Nike to take sneaker marketing to the next level, focusing on both the functional and the emotional jobs that customers are trying to get done. Of course this progression only makes sense in an industry that creates products and services that have the potential to define the customer's persona.

How Does the Sales Force Have Immediate Impact on Revenue Generation?

Many sales strategies specifically direct the sales team to uncover the customer's "needs" and then offer the solution that satisfies those needs. But as we have seen, a conventional approach to those tasks is likely to obtain ambiguous information from customers and will therefore result in a misguided sales pitch that pushes unwanted features or benefits, if it doesn't recommend the wrong product altogether. If, on the other hand, the sales team begins with a solid knowledge of the customer's outcomes and ascertains which are underserved, it can then create a sales pitch and solution that will connect with the customer front and center—with the result being a sale.

A number of outcome-driven companies provide their sales team with a simple tool that enables the team to put the segmentation findings to work. The salespeople are typically instructed to contact the customer of interest (a big or otherwise attractive account) and to ask the customer questions that allow the sales team to accurately determine which outcome-based segment (defined using the methods in Chapter 4) the customers fall into. This gives the sales team useful information that can guide sales activity. If, for example, a salesperson from a drug-infusion-pump manufacturer knows in advance that the customer he or she is about to visit belongs to the "programming-challenged" segment, then the salesperson can make a sales pitch that emphasizes the simplicity and value of the pump's programming features. The questions and algorithm needed to conduct this questioning and make the correct placement can be built into an Excel spreadsheet and become a road tool for the sales team.

What Is the Advantage of an Outcome-Based Brand?

Companies have discovered that outcome-driven thinking provides a solid foundation for a unique and powerful type of branding. Unlike a traditional brand, an outcome-based brand focuses the consumer's mind on the job the product or service will do for them. In other words, it connects the product to the job. For example, the power-tool manufacturer Milwaukee has created an effective outcome-based brand called the Sawzall for its line of reciprocating saws. Unlike a circular saw, a reciprocating saw cuts with a blade that goes back and forth in a traditional handsaw motion. Electricians, plumbers, and those in demolition often need such a tool to help them with the job of cutting through wood, metal, nails, drywall, and other construction materials they encounter. Milwaukee positioned its brand to capitalize on this job and designed its Sawzall to cut though just about anything. For more than twenty years, the Sawzall has dominated this market, and the name is often generically used to describe any reciprocating saw.

It is hard to match the strength of outcome-based brands. With them, customers know exactly what jobs the product will help them get done, which reduces confusion when making purchase decisions. A cleverly conceived brand name that connects the product to the job can make customers think of the product whenever they think about getting the job done—so much so that the product and the job may come to be thought of simultaneously. This can only happen when companies take an outcome-based approach to branding and sales.

Summary

Once a company has targeted the underserved outcomes that represent the best opportunities for growth and innovation, they are able to exploit those opportunities and gain revenue by selling more of the products and services they already offer. They accomplish this by better communicating and exploiting any advantages their products have in satisfying the targeted underserved outcomes. If a current product or service satisfies one or more underserved outcomes well, then a solid messaging strategy can inform customers of these advantages. The messaging strategy that is most effective clearly states a product's advantage in areas of the market that are highly underserved.

For a messaging strategy to achieve perfect alignment between the company and their customers, several conditions must be met. The company must:

- Be aware of the opportunities that exist—that is, know which outcomes are underserved
- Have a product that truly addresses the underserved outcomes
- Recognize what product features specifically address the underserved outcomes
- Determine if and where the current messaging is off

Breakdowns are common at each step of this process, resulting in faulty positioning and messaging strategies and slow sales.

When it comes to messaging, companies must decide whether they should base their messaging strategies on the functional jobs and outcomes their customers are trying to achieve or if they should also consider messaging along an emotional dimension. It is easier to make this decision if companies consider where their products fall in the functional-emotional matrix, with functional messaging being more appropriate for functionally complex products with low emotional appeal (such as medical devices and financial services) and both functional and emotional messaging being suitable for products that define the customer's persona (such as clothing and automobiles).

This chapter also introduces the idea of branding products to reflect the job they are helping people get done. In the reciprocating saw market, for example, Milwaukee has the Sawzall brand, a name that reflects the job the customer is trying to get done—namely, sawing through anything he or she should encounter. When companies use the brand name to link the product to the job being done, it makes people think about the brand every time they think about the job—creating a lasting impression.

Prioritizing Projects in the Development Pipeline

Separating the Winners from the Losers

- *What issues do companies face when prioritizing projects?*
- *What method is used to identify the winners and the losers?*
- *Which efforts should get top priority?*
- *What other factors affect project prioritization?*

With increasingly competitive pressures and tightened budgets, companies cannot afford to continue to bet on dozens of initiatives in the hopes that at least a few will succeed. A new method for prioritizing development initiatives is needed: one that can identify the initiatives that will create the most customer value and company profit.

In the last chapter we described how companies can generate net new growth in their existing product lines by alerting customers to the underserved outcomes those products satisfy—thereby communicating the products' true value. This is a good way to generate short-term growth because it requires only changes in messaging and not in the products themselves. To extend growth into the middle term, an outcome-driven company must assess the dozens of projects in its development pipeline and determine which products, features, ideas, and initiatives do the best job of addressing the remaining targeted underserved outcomes. Having identified them, a company must then commit the resources needed to get them to market quickly.

As discussed earlier, that is just what the angioplasty balloon manufacturer Cordis did when it recognized that the stent, which was one of about forty projects in its pipeline, specifically addressed its most important underserved outcome—minimizing the likelihood that blood vessels that have undergone angioplasty treatment will become narrowed once again. Cordis redirected development resources and threw its energies into getting the stent to market before any competitor could. The company succeeded, and Cordis led the market.

This chapter describes the seventh step in the outcome-driven innovation process, one that companies use to prioritize the products and services they have in the development pipeline. The theory behind the methodology is straight forward; products and services that satisfactorily address targeted market opportunities (by addressing underserved customer outcomes) are given high priority and the resources to get to market quickly. Those that fail to address targeted opportunities are reconsidered and often abandoned. Using this approach, companies are able to achieve three important business objectives simultaneously. They can deliver winning products that customers want, get valued products to market more quickly, and reduce unnecessary development expense. The result is an operational competitive advantage—more winning products on the market in less time and at less cost.

What Issues Do Companies Face When Prioritizing Projects?

We typically find that companies have far more development initiatives under way than they ever intended. It is not uncommon to see a company have from 20 to 200 projects in various stages of development. A poor filtering process often fails to weed out weak ideas and concepts. In studying how companies typically prioritize projects in the development pipeline, we have found that companies struggle with prioritizing projects because they:

- Have difficulty determining which concepts will address market opportunities
- Feel compelled to cover all bases so they do not get caught off guard
- Find it hard to kill a project once it has been funded
- Fail to assign the resources needed to get the projects to market quickly

These problems can be largely eliminated by applying the outcome-driven approach to innovation.

Difficulty Determining Which Concepts Will Address Market Opportunities

This difficulty stems directly from not knowing what market opportunities exist in the first place. Most companies do not know their customers' desired outcomes (certainly not all their desired outcomes) or which of those outcomes are most underserved. As a result, companies are forced to apply other methods to prioritize their projects. They try to make educated guesses, often giving most credence to inputs from the sales team, who think they know what features are needed to keep up with the competition. Often too, companies bend to the wills of executives and champions who are pushing their pet projects. They may react to competitors' new launches, diverting resources from their own potentially breakthrough initiatives, even though they do not know for sure that their competitors are targeting real opportunities.

Compulsion to Cover All Bases

Because companies don't know where opportunities exist in a market, they often feel compelled to invest in an excessive number of initiatives in the hope that at least some of these bets will succeed. They believe that this strategy will minimize the risk of being left behind or getting blindsided by a competitor. If a competitor is investing in a certain area, companies often feel compelled to make a similar investment, not because they know the competitor is doing the right thing, but because they do not know with certainty that the competitor is doing the wrong thing. When a seemingly good idea is brought forth by a respected project champion or a well placed executive, companies feel compelled to fund the project, not because they know with certainty that the resulting product will resonate with customers, but because they cannot say with confidence that the resulting product is likely to fail and is unworthy of funding.

This strategy comes with a high price tag. Being forced to place many bets drains company resources as it floods the development pipeline with a torrent of ideas—each of which takes dedication and energy to pursue.

Difficulty Killing Projects

Much has been written about how hard it is to kill projects in development. In a February 2003 *Harvard Business Review* article entitled "Why Bad Projects Are So Hard to Kill," professor of management Isabelle Royer says that many projects are hard to kill because of a "fervent and widespread belief among managers in the inevitability of their project's ultimate success." According to Royer, the desire to believe in something is primal. The excitement and exuberance associated with a project typically originate with the project champion, a person whose unyielding conviction that the project will succeed is often based on a hunch rather than on strong evidence. The champion's exuberance spreads because others also want to believe, especially if the champion is charismatic and well networked within the company. As a result, this sentiment spreads throughout the organization, often to the highest levels, reinforcing itself each step of the way. It is this dynamic that makes it hard to kill a project, even when there are signs that it will likely fail. Managers are slow to pull the plug because they believe that with a bit more work and investment the project will ultimately succeed.

Failure to Allocate Sufficient Resources to Get the Project to Market Quickly

Because companies tend to fund far more projects than they should, they are forced to spread limited resources across many projects. In the end, few projects receive the resources and attention they need to move forward quickly. Instead, they limp along, leaving the door open to a fast-moving competitor. This undisciplined approach to innovation costs *Fortune* 1000 companies more than $50 billion per year in wasted development expense and directs resources away from opportunities that are truly worthy of pursuit.

What Method Is Used to Identify the Winners and the Losers?

The method we have developed to prioritize products in the development pipeline require that a company:

- Have a clear understanding of customers' desired outcomes
- Know which outcomes are most important and least satisfied
- Identify and target the opportunities to pursue

Chapters 1 though 5 described how to get to this stage of the innovation process. Now, with the needed information in hand, the project prioritization process can begin.

The evaluation process has four basic steps. First, the company must determine what projects and initiatives to evaluate; second, it must select a team to complete the evaluation; third, the team must evaluate the initiatives; and fourth, the team must assess the results.

Determining What Projects and Initiatives to Evaluate

All the projects and initiatives in the pipeline that are aimed at the targeted market should be considered as part of the evaluation set. The initiatives may include full-blown product replacements, next-generation technologies, simple add-on features, or any other idea or concept that is currently receiving funding. It is possible that a new feature may address a number of the underserved outcomes and that a full-blown product replacement may fail to address any at all, in which case development of the feature would be accelerated while development of the product replacement might well be halted.

Selecting a Team to Complete the Evaluation

To conduct the evaluation, companies typically assemble a diversified team of competent and objective individuals from different functions within the company (research and development, marketing, and sales), as well as individuals from outside the firm (advisers, customers, and partners). The objective in selecting team members is to ensure that opposing views will be aired. You do not want a project champion to be the only person to evaluate his or her project.

Evaluating the Initiatives

One initiative at a time is evaluated for its ability to satisfy each underserved outcome: for each outcome, the team estimates the satisfaction rating customers would give the initiative. Specifically, the team asks the question, "What percentage of the customer population would rate their satisfaction a 4 or a 5 on a 5-point scale, where 5 means extremely satisfied and 1 means not satisfied at all?" If they conclude that 50 percent of the customer population would rate the outcome a 4 or a 5, then the outcome receives a satisfaction rating of 5.0. If they conclude that 75 percent would rate it a 4 or a 5, then it receives a satisfaction rating of 7.5, and so on.

Let's turn to Table 7.1 where we offer an example of a drug-pump manufacturer who evaluated four initiatives—two that are new features and two that are new products. The outcomes and numbers have been fictionalized so that competitors do not obtain valued information. Remember that although there may be 50 to

Table 7.1 Project Prioritization

| | | | | Ratings (sat) | | | |
| | | | | Feature Initiatives | | Product Initiatives | |
Desired outcomes for a drug pump	Imp	Sat	Opp	F1	F2	P1	P2
Minimize the amount of drug wasted when setting up the pump	9.3	4.2	14.4	4.2	4.2	3.8	**7.3**
Minimize the time it takes to figure out the size of the loading dose	9.3	5.3	13.3	5.3	5.3	4.6	**6.9**
Minimize the time it takes to validate the contents of the reservoir	8.6	4.4	12.8	4.4	4.4	4.4	**6.2**
Increase the accuracy with which the pump infuses	9.5	6.9	12.1	6.9	6.9	6.5	**7.9**
Minimize the frequency with which the medication must be replaced	8.7	5.7	11.7	**7.8**	5.7	6.6	6.8
Minimize the likelihood of mistakes when changing drug concentrations	8.5	5.5	11.5	5.5	5.5	5.5	**6.5**
Minimize the time it takes to determine the cause of an alarm	8.3	6.2	10.4	6.2	**7.5**	6.2	6.3
	Sat = 38.2			40.3	39.5	37.7	47.9

150 desired outcomes, the company is targeting only a handful for growth and innovation, so only those few are shown here. They all have high opportunity scores because only the most underserved outcomes were targeted.

The team first evaluates how well they believe the first new feature (feature 1—a larger medication reservoir) satisfies the desire to minimize the amount of drug wasted when setting up the pump. If one or two people on the team conclude that feature 1 would increase the satisfaction level to 5.6, for example, they must explain to the rest of the team why they believe this feature would generate more satisfaction than the 4.2 earned by current products (shown in column 4). A team member suggesting that feature 1 would generate a lower level of satisfaction than current products would also have to state the rationale behind his or her evaluation. In the end, the team reaches a consensus on the rating. In this case the team concluded that the larger medication reservoir did not impact the customer's ability to minimize the amount of drug wasted when setting up the pump, so they assigned the feature the same rating as that earned by current products: 4.2.

Next, the team evaluates how well they believe feature 1 satisfies the customer's desire to minimize the time it takes to figure out the size of the loading dose, which is the second targeted outcome on the list. They follow the same procedure until they have evaluated feature 1 against all the targeted outcomes. It turns out that the only outcome for which the team estimates that the larger reservoir will increase customer satisfaction is minimizing the frequency with which the medication must be replaced. For that outcome the team agrees that the satisfaction level would be greatly increased, and they assign feature 1 a rating of 7.8. Feature 2, product 1, and product 2 are then evaluated in the same fashion. Any time the team gives an initiative a rating higher than that of current offerings, the team must state what unique feature or attribute accounts for the higher rating. This helps bring objectivity to the evaluation process.

Assessing the Results

The results for product initiatives are assessed differently than the results for feature initiatives. Product initiatives are expected to impact a good number of outcomes; in fact a well-conceptualized product would address all the underserved outcomes. In Table 7.1 we see that product 1 does a poor job of addressing the targeted outcomes, and, in fact, the team has estimated that it will provide less overall satisfaction (37.7) than the currently available products (38.2). Product 2, on the other hand, does a great job of addressing the targeted outcomes and achieves an overall rating of 47.9. (The overall rating is simply the sum of the satisfaction scores given to each outcome. More complex algorithms can be used that take weighted opportunity into consideration, but to simplify the discussion I have chosen to discuss only this most elementary scoring method.) We can conclude from this simple evaluation that product 2 should receive continued and even accelerated funding while product 1 should be killed.

Unlike a new product, a new feature is not likely to impact many outcomes. Therefore, when assessing a feature, it makes more sense to look at the feature's ability to address specific targeted outcomes than to look at the feature's overall score. For example, feature 1— the larger reservoir—only impacts the customer's ability to minimize the frequency with which the medication must be replaced, but it addresses that outcome extremely well. Likewise, feature 2, which happens to be an intricate method for translating error codes into a language that can be quickly understood by nurses, has a very positive impact on minimizing the time it takes to determine the cause of an alarm. Both these features deserve continued funding because they deliver exceptional customer value.

In addition, if we take a closer look at product 2, we see that it does not do a good job of minimizing the frequency with which the medication must be replaced or of minimizing the time it takes to determine the cause of an alarm. Therefore, the developers should consider adding features 1 and 2 to product 2, as doing so would deliver significant additional customer value. This is the type of strategic thinking and planning that often follows the completion of a pipeline evaluation.

If a company finds that a specific initiative does a great job of addressing a major opportunity, as Cordis did when evaluating the stent, then giving that initiative top priority makes sense because the result may be the creation of a new, high-margin product. If a company finds that an initiative could be vastly improved with some minor changes, as in the drug pump example above, then those changes should be included and funded. If a company finds that certain initiatives fail to address the targeted opportunities, then their funding should be halted. There may be many possibilities, but the objective remains the same: determine which initiatives deliver value and get those to market quickly.

Which Efforts Should Get Top Priority?

With a targeted set of outcomes in the crosshairs, a company is able to make several important determinations relating to pipeline prioritization. They are able to validate which products or initiatives are currently underway:

- Do the best job of addressing the targeted, underserved outcomes
- Fail to address the targeted outcomes
- Address outcomes that are unimportant and/or already overserved

In addition, they are able to determine what potential competitive products are causes for concern, fueling the formulation of an effective competitive strategy.

Suppose that a manufacturer of drug-infusion pumps identified minimizing the amount of drug that is wasted when the pump is set up, minimizing the time it takes to determine the size of a loading dose, and minimizing the time it takes to validate the contents of the pump reservoir as being among the key underserved outcomes. The manufacturer would first look at the projects in its pipeline to see which ones satisfied those outcomes best. This analysis would simultaneously reveal which initiatives fail to address the opportunities. Upon completing such an evaluation, managers would be able to predict with a high degree of certainty which projects and initiatives will hit the targets and are worthy of continued or even accelerated funding.

As an example of this type of analysis, Table 7.2, which replaces the initiatives shown in Table 7.1 with four other product initiatives, shows a fictionalized evaluation of the projects of a certain drug-

Table 7.2 Identifying the Best Initiatives

				Ratings (sat)			
Desired outcomes for a drug pump	Imp	Sat	Opp	#1	#2	#3	#4
Minimize the amount of drug wasted when setting up the pump	9.3	4.2	14.4	7.3	3.2	3.8	6.2
Minimize the time it takes to figure out the size of the loading dose	9.3	5.3	13.3	6.9	4.8	4.6	6.7
Minimize the time it takes to validate the contents of the reservoir	8.6	4.4	12.8	6.2	4.4	4.4	6.1
Increase the accuracy with which the pump infuses	9.5	6.9	12.1	7.9	6.7	6.5	7.4
Minimize the frequency with which the medication must be replaced	8.7	5.7	11.7	6.8	5.5	6.6	5.8
Minimize the likelihood of mistakes when changing drug concentrations	8.5	5.5	11.5	6.5	5.2	5.5	5.8
Minimize the time it takes to determine the cause of an alarm	8.3	6.2	10.4	6.2	6.2	8.7	6.2

pump manufacturer. They see that initiative 1 does a good job of increasing the satisfaction levels of nearly all the targeted outcomes, initiative 2 fails to address any of the targeted outcomes, initiative 3 does a great job of satisfying just one targeted outcome (the last one in the list), and initiative 4 (a competitive product that is expected shortly from a competitor) is worthy of concern as it does a good job of satisfying several of the top opportunities. Let's look at each situation in more detail.

What Initiatives Do the Best Job of Addressing the Targeted Outcomes?

The initiatives that satisfy the highest-priority targeted outcomes are the ones that are most likely to generate customer value and company revenue. It is not uncommon for companies to find one or two projects in the pipeline that indeed hit those targets, as Cordis did with the stent. Usually, though, those projects have been languishing and underfunded among the many initiatives in the pipeline. Once the company recognizes these projects' value, however, they should back them wholeheartedly and accelerate their funding, as being first to market may become a critical factor in the company's ultimate success.

When conducting the analysis, companies generally give initiatives that satisfy the most high-opportunity outcomes a higher priority than those that address only one or two outcomes. If, for example, the drug-infusion pump manufacturer found that one initiative dramatically improved the satisfaction of all the targeted outcomes, then that initiative would receive accelerated funding and more resources. Initiatives that satisfy a single outcome with a high opportunity score typically receive a higher priority than those that satisfy a single outcome with a lower opportunity score. Cost, risk, and effort also factor into the prioritization algorithm. If two initiatives both address the same opportunities, then the one that adds the least product cost, requires the least amount of effort, and presents the least technical risk will take priority.

What Initiatives Fail to Address the Targeted Outcomes?

Not all the products in the pipeline will address the targeted opportunities, but some will be more off target than others. Keep in mind, the targeted opportunities may not include all the opportunities that exist in the market, just those that represent the greatest opportunity for growth. Some pipeline initiatives, then, may be aimed at addressing what we can call second-tier opportunities, those, for example, with opportunity scores in the range of 10 to 11. These are opportunities that will eventually need to be addressed in the market, but not before the big opportunities are addressed. Companies should reduce funding to initiatives that are focused on outcomes such as these until a later date. Alternatively, the concept can be tweaked to address the key opportunities or combined with another initiative if the combination will produce a valuable result.

Other initiatives, however, may be even further off the mark because they fail to address even these second-tier opportunities. Generally speaking, projects aimed at outcomes that have opportunity scores of less than 10 fall into this category. Companies should consider abandoning those initiatives as they will fail to deliver even minimal customer value now or in the future.

What Initiatives Address Unimportant or Overserved Outcomes?

It is common to find that some pipeline initiatives are totally off the mark, addressing outcomes that are just not important to the target market or that are already well satisfied. In either case the initiative is simply a waste of the company's time and resources and should be abandoned. Anywhere from 10 to 25 percent of a company's initiatives are likely to fall into this category, and eliminating them can translate into millions of dollars in development expense saved.

If an outcome is unimportant (and to us that means 20 percent or fewer customers rate it a 4 or a 5 for importance, even in the most demanding segment), it will never be an area in which additional value creation is possible. That aspect of getting the job done is simply not important to customers, and making it better is just not an attractive or necessary proposition. In fact, improvements would likely lead to a more costly but not a more valued product.

If an outcome is already overserved, which is to say more satisfied than it is important, then additional value creation is not possible. Customers are already satisfied enough; they are not willing to pay more to be more satisfied. If a food product that is 99.5 percent fat free costs a dollar, then customers will be unlikely to pay half again as much for an improved product that is 99.9 percent fat free. Companies need to know when to stop improving along a specific dimension.

Knowing with certainty that an initiative is targeted at unimportant or overserved outcomes gives executives the ammunition they need to get past project exuberance and the project champion's belief in the inevitability of the project's ultimate success. Even the most talented engineers and designers cannot deliver value where none is desired.

What Potential Competitive Products Are Cause for Concern?

By evaluating the products and services a company believes its competitors have on the horizon, the company can determine if any competitive products in the works are likely to address big opportunities, if and where competitors have weaknesses, and if a competitor is focused on unimportant or overserved outcomes. In the last case, knowing that the competitor is focused on outcomes that will not generate any value makes it easy to resist the urge to imitate.

If it is discovered that a competitor is soon going to introduce a product that addresses a key opportunity, then that knowledge is likely to affect project prioritization. Because a quick counter response may be needed, the highest priority may be given to a comparable initiative—one that allows the company to catch up quickly. With a solid competitive assessment in hand a company knows where to lead and when to follow—and when to run away.

What Other Factors Affect Project Prioritization?

When several competing initiatives are found to address many of the underserved outcomes, each initiative may also be evaluated for factors such as effort and risk, with the initiative that delivers the most overall value for the least effort and risk receiving the higher priority. Product cost and competitive sustainability are also often used as additional evaluation criteria.

When all of a company's competitors satisfy an important outcome better than the company itself, then the company should give high priority to an initiative that helps overcome that competitive weakness even if the outcome was not one that the company had originally targeted. The outcome will not show up as underserved in an analysis of the market because it is not underserved by most companies—only by the company in question. Addressing this weakness may mean reprioritizing projects in the pipeline.

Sometimes a company may find itself faced with a new regulatory constraint. For example, if it should be decided that all voting machines must provide a paper trail, that new requirement would affect manufacturers' project prioritization. Compliance efforts would receive top priority, possibly overriding other initiatives in the pipeline.

Lastly, companies may also choose to evaluate pipeline initiatives against internal company stakeholder outcomes. For example, one initiative may be better than another because it will enable a company to minimize the time it takes to enter an important market or increase the sales of existing products. In many industries it is common for a company to consider up to fifty stakeholder outcomes.

Summary

Once a company knows what opportunities to target, it can generate net new growth in its existing product lines by alerting customers to the underserved outcomes its products satisfy—thereby communicating the products' true value. To generate additional growth, the company must determine which of the initiatives in its product development pipeline do the best job of addressing the remaining targeted underserved outcomes. The objective is to bring those initiatives to market quickly and to abandon initiatives that fail to create additional customer value. When prioritizing is done effectively, companies can achieve three important business objectives simultaneously. They can deliver winning products that customers want, get valued products to market more quickly, and reduce unnecessary development expense.

Unfortunately, many companies:

- Have difficulty determining which concepts will address market opportunities
- Feel compelled to cover all bases so they do not get caught off guard
- Find it hard to kill a project once it has been funded
- Fail to assign the resources needed to get projects to market quickly

The solution is to take an outcome-based approach to project prioritization. Managers must identify the projects that do the best job of addressing targeted underserved outcomes, as well as those that fail to address the targeted outcomes and those that address outcomes that are unimportant or overserved. Upon completing such an evaluation, managers can predict with a high degree of certainty which projects and initiatives are worthy of continued or even accelerated funding. The evaluation process has four basic steps. First, the company must determine what projects and initiatives to evaluate; second, the company must select a team to complete the evaluation; third, the team must evaluate the initiatives; and fourth, the team must assess the results. Such an evaluation results in a list of initiatives prioritized based on their ability to deliver value to the customer and revenue to the firm.

Devising Breakthrough Concepts

Using Focused Brainstorming and the Customer Scorecard to Create Customer Value

- *Why does traditional brainstorming often fail to produce breakthrough ideas?*
- *How are breakthrough concepts successfully generated?*
- *What are the mechanics behind focused brainstorming?*
- *Why do traditional concept-evaluation methods fail?*
- *How is the customer scorecard used to evaluate product and service concepts?*
- *How are these methods applied in practice?*
- *What is the role of R&D in the innovation process?*

As described in Chapters 6 and 7, once a set of opportunities are identified and targeted in a market, a company works to tackle those opportunities first by optimizing its messaging strategy and exploiting the advantages its current products have in seizing those opportunities and then by prioritizing its development pipeline so it can quickly bring to market those products and services that do the best job of addressing the remaining targeted opportunities. These two steps will result in increased sales and new growth, but the job of value creation is not yet complete. There is no guarantee that a company's existing products and those it has in its pipeline address all or even any of the opportunities that have been identified and targeted, especially if the company is new to the market. Additional actions will almost certainly be required. To address the remaining opportunities, a company must either think of new, potentially breakthrough products and product features that satisfy the remaining underserved outcomes or acquire technology through licensing or acquisition that will make it possible for the company to satisfy the targeted outcomes.

When Cordis Corporation targeted fifteen underserved outcomes in the angioplasty balloon market, they discovered that their current products and those they had in their development pipeline addressed only a handful of those outcomes. To become the market leader the company had to devise a new set of product features that addressed the remaining dozen or so underserved outcomes. Through focused idea generation, they did just that, and eighteen months later they released a line of angioplasty balloon products that catapulted their market share from 5 to 20 percent.

This chapter describes how outcome-driven companies deal with the remaining unexploited opportunities using advanced methods for idea generation and idea evaluation. It introduces what we call focused brainstorming, a new approach to idea generation that challenges conventional wisdom. With focused brainstorming, ideation is simplified, eliminating much of the unnecessary complexity and process variability introduced with traditional methods. As for idea evaluation, in this chapter we introduce the "customer scorecard," an outcome-based idea evaluation method that makes it possible to quantify the amount of value a new idea is likely to deliver and how its value delivery compares with that of current and competitive products. The customer scorecard makes it possible for companies to determine if a proposed idea or concept is likely to succeed or fail in advance of any development effort. With that knowledge, companies can make sure that only those initiatives that promise to create customer value enter the development pipeline to begin with.

Why Does Traditional Brainstorming Often Fail to Produce Breakthrough Ideas?

Most brainstorming and idea generation efforts yield poor and un-actionable results for three key reasons. The first is because managers rarely know how or where to direct employees' creative energy. The result is much wasted energy, hundreds of useless ideas, and, unfortunately, few ideas that are truly worthy of pursuit. Consider the typical pattern. In most firms, when employees are asked to come up with new ideas, they are not directed to focus on specific outcomes; rather, they are asked for ideas to improve the company's products in general (function, ergonomics, fit and finish, distribution, and packaging), leaving the direction for improvement open to interpretation. In the absence of a specific target, employees in turn focus on what they themselves want to improve rather than on what customers want to see improved. This scattershot approach to idea generation will not yield a bull's-eye because there is no target to aim for.

Let's suppose that medical professionals who use drug pumps are unsatisfied with the amount of drug that is wasted when setting up currently available pumps and with the accuracy with which current pumps infuse. If employees of a drug-pump manufacturer are unaware of those dissatisfactions, then they will have no idea that those are outcomes on which they should focus their creative energies. Instead, they may be spending their time trying to figure out how to make the pump smaller or how to make it pump faster, even though customers may not be interested in improvements in those areas.

Despite this lack of focus, employees do come up with ideas—hundreds of them, in fact. And that is the cause of the second problem; companies often measure the success of an ideation session by the number of ideas that are generated, not the quality of those ideas. Third-party firms contribute to this exuberance for idea generation as they encourage unfocused ideation efforts whose aim is to bring forth hundreds of ideas. Should success be declared when a company comes up with 400 ideas? 500 ideas? What is the right number? Will hundreds of ideas guarantee success? Not at all. We contend that measuring the number of ideas generated by employees and others is not only the wrong measure of success, but a misleading measure as well.

The third problem arises because so many ideas exist and most companies lack a useful way to evaluate them. Because managers rarely know what customer outcomes are underserved, they are unable to recognize a good idea when they see it. Instead, they rely on random and often irrelevant criteria in evaluating ideas and may decide to pursue an initiative because it is snazzy, sexy, or otherwise interesting—without knowing if and how the idea creates customer value. As has been true of every other aspect of innovation that we have discussed, the solution to this problem is to know what jobs customers are trying to do and what outcomes they are trying to achieve.

How Are Breakthrough Concepts Successfully Generated?

From our perspective, companies do not need to generate hundreds of ideas. Rather they need only to generate a handful of ideas that specifically and satisfactorily address the customer's underserved desired outcomes. This in effect flips the innovation process on its head. Instead of thinking up ideas and then trying to figure out which ideas merit value, we believe that companies should only generate ideas around the underserved outcomes, guaranteeing that the time spent doing so will result in ideas that are worthy of pursuit. Why waste time thinking about how to better satisfy outcomes that are unimportant or overserved?

Until now, the key ingredient to successful idea generation has been missing: a target. Unless a corn seed manufacturer knows with certainty, for example, that 85 percent of corn farmers say that increasing the percentage of plants that emerge at the same time is both very important to them and not well satisfied by currently available corn seed, then it is unlikely to be able to point its development teams in the right direction. Knowing where to focus creativity is the key to successful and accountable innovation. To successfully generate breakthrough solutions, companies must identify and address their customers' most underserved outcomes and do so in a way that does not diminish performance along other important dimensions.

We often like to ask, "How many people within your organization know all the outcomes that customers are trying to achieve?" If your firm is like most, the answer will be "none." We also like to ask, "Of those that know what outcomes customers want to achieve (if any), how many know which outcomes are most underserved?" Here again the typical answer is "none." Although the employee population as a whole may collectively understand the customer's outcomes, this information is rarely documented, prioritized, or shared throughout the firm. CEOs must then ask, "How can I expect my business units to consistently produce blockbuster products and services when no one individual or function knows what outcomes are underserved and overserved, or how they are prioritized?"

In a complete turnaround, when working in an outcome-driven environment, all employees are able to share in that knowledge and use it to focus on the creation of value, collectively contributing to the systematic creation of breakthrough solutions. Imagine the impact on an organization's ability to innovate when the number of employees that know how customers measure value increases from less than 1 percent to nearly 100 percent, and when all key employees know where to focus their creativity and know how to quantify the value of an idea.

In our experience, if companies know those underserved outcomes, they are able to devise highly valued solutions more than 90 percent of the time. Organizational issues may interfere with successful execution, lowering the overall success rate, but valued ideas are consistently generated. Here we defined "highly valued" as ideas that improve the customer satisfaction level of an underserved outcome by 20 percent or more. Such a high success rate should not come as a great surprise, because companies are rarely lacking creative people and new ideas—what they are typically lacking is direction. Whether one considers Bosch's innovations with the circular saw or AIG's innovations in the insurance market, it is clear that once the target was known, the companies were fully capable of hitting it. In the words of Paul Zarookian, executive vice president of AIG's A.I. Imperial Financing division, "Knowing where to focus our creativity made all the difference in the world. In a two-day idea generation session we generated new ideas for operational process changes and Web-based services that addressed the underserved outcomes. As important, knowing where the market was overserved prevented us from expending resources on service functions our agents would deem of little value. Because we had solid targets for ideation, we were able to devise a breakthrough solution, which has provided us with a competitive advantage."

As generally happens when using this approach, the A.I. Imperial team made several worthwhile observations as they worked their way through the idea-generation session. First, they recognized that many of the ideas they generated did not require new technology or invention; rather, they were clever applications of existing technology, focused on satisfying specific customer outcomes. This helped to dispel the myth that innovation is dependent on the creation of new technology.

Second, they observed that their breakthrough solution was not the result of any one big idea or feature; it was the result of many ideas or features being brought together and collectively adding significant value to the overall offering—without inadvertently diluting value along other important dimensions.

What Are the Mechanics Behind Focused Brainstorming?

With a diverse team of employees engaged in ideation, a company can generate ideas that target opportunities that neither its current products nor those in its pipeline address. The approach works best when companies follow the five guidelines we have developed to control process variability and ensure a successful result:

- Stay focused on the targets
- Aim for breakthrough improvement
- Constrain thinking to enhance creativity
- Eliminate bad ideas quickly
- Optimize the best idea for cost, effort, risk, and sustainability

Stay Focused on the Targets

The first rule is to keep the ideation team focused on generating ideas that specifically address the high-opportunity outcomes. Do not let them wander off course and push ideas that are focused on satisfying other, less important outcomes. It is common, especially early on in an ideation session, to see participants push ideas that they have long held dear even if those ideas do not address the outcome at hand. When employees of a drug-infusion-pump manufacturer were asked to figure out a way to minimize the amount of drug wasted when setting up the pump, for example, one employee suggested that they increase the capacity of the drug container. This idea, as it turns out, was one the employee had suggested in the past and wanted to see accepted. Although a larger drug container addressed another outcome, minimizing the frequency with which the medication must be replaced, it did not specifically address the targeted outcome. To reach this conclusion, the team was asked, "If you were to increase the capacity of the drug container, to what degree would you minimize the amount of drug wasted when setting up the pump?" The team quickly realized that the size of the drug container had little bearing on this outcome, so they set the idea aside and refocused their ideation efforts on the targeted outcome.

To help maintain the needed focus, outcomes are typically addressed one at a time. An exception is when several related outcomes can be grouped into an outcome theme that allows all the outcomes to be addressed at once. If several outcomes related to controlling the drug dose, for example, could potentially be addressed with one idea, they are grouped into a theme for ideation. Creating themes in this manner cuts down on the number of features that must be added to a product to address the underserved outcomes, which helps keep the product cost down.

Aim for Breakthrough Improvement

When brainstorming, employees are instructed to devise ideas that make significant improvements in customer satisfaction, not just incremental improvements. Most underserved outcomes are characterized by satisfaction levels of less than 5.0, meaning less than 50 percent of customers rate their satisfaction level for that outcome on the high end (4 or 5) of a 1-to-5 scale. We suggest that the ideation team attempt to generate ideas that deliver a satisfaction level of 8.0 or higher; that is, ideas that will result in 80 percent of the customers reaching satisfaction levels of 4 or 5. Achieving such a high satisfaction level is historically difficult and often requires new thinking. We often suggest lateral thinking, TRIZ rules (TRIZ, the theory of inventive problem solving, is a systematic approach to ideation originally developed in the Soviet Union in the 1940s that became popular in certain big-name U.S. companies in the 1990s), and other methods to help generate ideas that are worthy of pursuit. Regardless of the methods used, the goal is to achieve breakthrough improvement. It is rare that a breakthrough idea is not produced within a couple of days.

Constrain Thinking to Enhance Creativity

When Bosch began their circular-saw ideation session, team members were told not only to generate ideas that solidly addressed the underserved outcomes but that also did not add any cost to the product. This was critical to the success of the CS20 circular saw because the saw had to compete at price points specified by Home Depot and Lowes. While some experts suggest that applying constraints is confining and may stifle creativity, we argue that on the contrary, constraints focus creativity in a way that generates valuable, usable, and practical ideas. Bosch's decision to remove the cord from the CS20 circular not only reduced production costs, making possible the addition of other features while keeping the final product at the desired price point, it also enabled the company to satisfy a number of underserved outcomes better, including customers' desires to minimize the frequency with which the cord must be replaced, minimize downtime when a cord is inadvertently cut, and minimize the cost of replacing a cut cord. Simultaneously reducing costs and adding value is clearly innovation.

Bosch also addressed two remaining underserved outcomes (minimizing the likelihood that users get debris in their eyes and minimizing the frequency with which the cut line cannot be seen) with a design change that did not add to the product's price. This was accomplished by redirecting the airflow coming out of the motor onto the cut path, pushing debris off the cut line and away from the user's face. Would Bosch have come up with these solutions without the cost constraint? It is doubtful—no one else in the industry had ever managed it. It appears from Bosch's experience that directing employees to honor cost, effort, or other restrictions when devising new solutions does not dilute the divergent-thinking process; it keeps it focused and within bounds.

Eliminate Bad Ideas Quickly

Whoever said there is no such thing as a bad idea has never participated in an idea generation session. There are plenty of bad ideas. These are ideas that are impractical and costly and that fail to address underserved outcomes. Outcome-driven companies eliminate these bad ideas quickly as they are evaluated immediately after they are generated. If the idea does not have the potential to significantly or totally satisfy 80 percent of the target customers (remember, the aim is breakthrough improvement), then the idea is eliminated. If the idea requires excessive time or resources it is either improved or eliminated. Killing bad ideas early saves time and expense, and it's also easier than waiting: the earlier the bad news comes, the more likely the originator of the idea will be able to let go of the idea without a struggle and refocus his or her thinking in a more positive direction.

Optimize the Best Idea for Cost, Effort, Risk, and Sustainability

The objective of outcome-driven ideation is not dozens of ideas; one or two really great ideas for each targeted outcome is what to aim for. The best idea will not only enable a company to achieve the desired 8.0 satisfaction level, it will also meet four important criteria. It will:

- Not add any product cost
- Require little effort to develop
- Present little technical risk
- Be difficult for a competitor to copy—which means that it will provide a sustainable advantage

Once the team has generated an idea that delivers the desired level of satisfaction, the team must then make whatever modifications are necessary in order for the idea to meet these four criteria. If the proposed idea requires a large effort, for example, the team is asked to devise an alternative idea that contributes similar value but can be executed with significantly less effort. To take a concrete example, when developing the CS20 circular saw, the Bosch team initially proposed a laser guidance system to address customers' desire to minimize the likelihood of the cut going off track—but that solution would have added too much cost to the saw. Instead, they came up with the idea of redirecting the blower to keep debris off the cut path. This did as good a job as the laser (if not better) at minimizing the likelihood that the saw would inadvertently go off track while making the cut.

Why Do Traditional Concept-Evaluation Methods Fail?

After the brainstorming sessions have been completed and the suggestion boxes have been emptied, companies are faced with the daunting task of sorting through hundreds of product and service ideas. The value of the ideas must be validated and quantified so the firm can move forward in its development with confidence and conviction. This presents a new set of challenges.

To gain a competitive advantage today, it is not enough for a company to *hope* that a new product or service will succeed once it is delivered; a company must *know* the new offering will succeed. To achieve this level of certainty, a company must not only determine whether or not a product idea will deliver customer value, the company must also know how much more value it will deliver than the products and services it is competing with. Ideally the company will know if the new offering satisfies the collective set of customer outcomes 5 percent more or 20 percent more.

But how should a company measure value? Among the more common concept evaluation methods are:

- Internal assessments
- Qualitative customer assessments
- Quantitative customer assessments
- Selective assessments

Each method and its shortcomings are worthy of a short discussion.

Internal Assessments

Companies that do not have the time, money, or ability to apply more elaborate concept evaluation methods may fall back on any number of simple internal-assessment methods. A company may simply see if the new offering fits the current business model, is easily justified from a financial perspective, or fits with the company's existing competencies and reject ideas that don't live up to the chosen standard. Because none of these methods takes customers' outcomes into account, they are as likely to reject a winning idea as to accept it.

We have seen many companies employ a simplified winnowing process that filters out those ideas that cannot be executed using the company's existing competencies. This approach is shortsighted, as this decision suggests the company is unwilling to master the new competencies needed to address any remaining opportunities for growth. In addition, a company that always plays to its strengths is likely to end up addressing outcomes that are already overserved.

Qualitative Customer Assessments

Companies that have greater resources may use qualitative customer assessments to evaluate their collection of potential new offerings. One common form of qualitative customer assessment is the focus group. In a focus group, a small number of customers are invited to discuss and comment on different product ideas and prototypes. This approach is riddled with problems.

First, customers are not consciously aware of all the outcomes they want to achieve. Most people can think of no more than nine criteria at a time against which to make an evaluation. With 50 to 150 outcomes commonplace, there is no way a customer can make a valid assessment of a product concept in a typical focus group environment. Drug-infusion-pump customers may say that they like a product because it helps them minimize the time it takes to program the pump, for example, but fail to recognize that the new programming feature inhibits their ability to minimize the likelihood of a drug overdose. Not seeing the new pump's shortcomings, they may give it a glowing review—but the marketplace will not be so kind.

In addition, customers may not be technically savvy enough to make an accurate product assessment. They may not make the connection between a new technology and its benefits, and therefore they may fail to recognize the value that a new technology offers. Consumers initially gave the microwave oven the thumbs down because they failed to understand and appreciate the technology.

Furthermore, even assuming that customer feedback will be valuable in some way, there is the problem of which ideas customers are asked to evaluate. Because customers cannot be asked to evaluate all the ideas that are swirling around a company, they are typically shown those ideas that the company thinks are most promising. That means some form of internal evaluation has already taken place, with all the problems associated with internal evaluations, as discussed above. Companies may assume they know which ideas are likely to be most attractive, but are they right? What if they have eliminated the best options and included only those that have intuitive appeal, are easy to implement, fit the current business model, or can be more easily justified from a financial perspective? Letting customers evaluate a few select solutions may help to determine which of those ideas are best, but it does not guarantee that the best of the bunch is highly valued. It too may be a poor solution—just better than the others.

Last, we find that customers rarely agree on which solution is best. This should not come as a surprise. Individuals in a focus group are likely to represent different segments of opportunity and will therefore measure value differently. Some may be overserved and some may be underserved. Attempting to reach consensus is futile. It just won't happen. Companies that rely on focus groups usually don't recognize this, however, and may modify their product concept in hopes of appealing to all customers. The result is likely to be suboptimal for all and valuable to none.

Quantitative Customer Assessments

Some companies use quantitative research methods (methods that generate numeric data) to obtain customer input on new product ideas. Customers may be asked to make paired product comparisons or to perform a constant-sum rating (distributing a fixed number of points among a group of competitive offerings). Unfortunately, because these methods, like the qualitative methods described above, still rely on the customer, they have the same fundamental shortcomings as the qualitative methods—for instance, customers will still be asked to rate a preselected group of products or ideas rather than the full array of possibilities. Conjoint analysis is a good example of this, as it is designed to test a product concept with a certain number of predefined features and looks to optimize the feature combinations at various price points. Although this may be helpful in certain situations (when the optimal feature set is already known), this approach alone rarely produces conclusive results.

Selective Assessments

Occasionally the winnowing process succumbs to politics and personal goals. A powerful executive, an aggressive engineer, or a convincing marketer who wants to see his or her product go to market may use carefully selected tidbits of data to "prove" that the product is the one that should be pursued. A product that is chosen in this manner rarely represents the best value for the customer.

None of these traditional evaluation methods is effective because they all fail to evaluate a product's potential to get a job done and address the customer's desired outcomes. Some companies don't even try to assess a product's value before it goes to market. Instead they assess a products' value after the fact, by seeing how much revenue it generates. This is an unforgiving approach if expectations are not met.

How Is the Customer Scorecard Used to Evaluate Product and Service Concepts?

In an outcome-driven environment, company team members, not customers, objectively judge proposed new products by determining the degree to which the proposed offering satisfies all the possible customer outcomes and quantifying the total value the offering delivers. This measurement is a leading indicator because customer satisfaction and value creation are predictive of revenue, growth, and success. Bosch, for example, knew that its CS20 circular saw would be a success before it came to market because it addressed the top ten unsatisfied customer outcomes. Initial market tests with Lowes and Home Depot showed Bosch's confidence to be well placed, as it did with customers themselves, once the saw was launched. This saw was also recognized by *Popular Science* as one of the top 100 innovations of 2004. The fact that it addressed many underserved outcomes was predictive of its ultimate success.

To begin evaluating how well a product idea or concept addresses customer outcomes for a specific job, all the outcomes (usually some 50 to 150 total) are listed in priority order from most to least underserved in a customer scorecard. Table 8.1 shows an abbreviated example of a customer scorecard. (A real scorecard would contain all 50 to 150 outcomes that have been collected.) Since the outcomes collectively represent 100 percent of the deliverable value, it is pos-

Table 8.1 The Customer Scorecard

Desired outcomes for a drug pump	Imp	Sat	Opp	Concept Ratings (sat)			
				C1	C2	C3	C4
Minimize the amount of drug wasted when setting up the pump	9.3	4.2	14.4	4.2	4.2	3.8	7.3
Minimize the time it takes to figure out the size of the loading dose	9.3	5.3	13.3	5.3	5.3	4.6	6.9
Minimize the time it takes to validate the contents of the reservoir	8.6	4.4	12.8	4.4	4.4	4.4	6.2
Increase the accuracy with which the pump infuses	9.5	6.9	12.1	6.9	6.9	6.5	7.9
Minimize the frequency with which the medication must be replaced	8.7	5.7	11.7	7.8	5.7	6.6	6.8
. . .							
Minimize the time it takes to determine the cause of an alarm	8.3	6.2	10.4	6.2	7.5	6.2	6.3
				40.3	39.5	37.7	47.9

sible to quantify the total amount of value any newly proposed idea or solution will deliver. It is possible, for example, to determine that one concept delivers 55 percent of the possible value while another concept delivers 65 percent. It is also possible to see how much value a new offering has relative to those already on the market. The product or concept that obtains the highest overall score is generally the one that will be chosen for pursuit.

Exceptions to this rule are possible. Competing concepts that deliver equal value are also often evaluated for other factors, such as effort and risk; in those cases, a concept that delivers less value but can be developed in far less time occasionally will be pursued and developed.

During the course of an evaluation a company may find that a newly proposed concept does a good job of addressing one or more top opportunities, but at the expense of other outcomes, and in total it delivers less value than a currently available solution. With this insight the company can refrain from pursuing the proposed concept, thereby avoiding an expensive mistake. A company will also be made aware of the weaknesses in its best concept and may go back and improve it.

When J. R. Simplot used this approach to improve their french fries, for example, they were able to eliminate several ideas from consideration and modify others that would deliver significant value. Business development manager Kim Westover says, "The ability to quantify our ideas against the customer's measures of value really changed our plans—in fact, it completely reordered our development priorities. Using this approach we were able to generate and validate exciting ideas that we never would have uncovered using traditional idea generation methods. Several ideas showed dramatic improvement over currently marketed products. One idea, which we had previously ignored, turned into a star project after we saw how it addressed many key opportunities for improvement across a large percentage of the market. The information collected as part of this effort clarified and substantiated precisely what actions our designers needed to take to create exciting products. As an important side benefit, time and energy formerly spent on lobbying was eliminated as project selection was based on the use of outcome-based tools and facts rather than on the salesmanship of a champion."

We often find that establishing a basis for agreement via the customer scorecard changes the dynamics of the ideation team and the cross-functional interaction. Instead of arguing over whose idea is best and using subjective data and opinion to support their positions, team members from marketing and development work together to determine which ideas best satisfy the outcomes and fine-tune those that are best.

Through years of experience using this measurement system in both manufacturing and service industries, we have been able to quantify just how much additional value must be created before a company can be confident that their new products or services will be a success. It turns out that products that deliver less than 3 percent more value than those currently available often fail. By contrast, most successful new products and services (defined here as products that maintain or incrementally grow a company's market share and/or revenue) typically deliver between 5 and 10 percent more value than currently available products. Product and service ideas that deliver 20 percent or more value often result in dramatic increases in market share, revenue, and profit. Cordis Corporation's angioplasty balloon product line, for example, improved overall customer satisfaction to about 40 percent to 50 percent, an improvement of approximately 25 percent. Their stent delivered about 100 percent more value, with customer satisfaction rising from 25 percent to about 50 percent.

How Are These Methods Applied in Practice?

For a look at how our outcome-driven approach to idea generation and concept evaluation works in practice, let's take the example of

Florida-based Pratt & Whitney (P&W), the government jet engine division of United Technologies. In 1994 the vice president of P&W's manufacturing services division was convinced that a planned, multimillion dollar expenditure on a shop floor logistical control system would generate significant new value for the division's customers. However, he wanted confirmation and broad management agreement before making the investment. The division was in effect an in-house design and manufacturing shop that produced machined parts for new jet engine designs. They catered mostly to P&W engineers, many of whom had taken their business to outside suppliers over recent years. Management was intent on winning that business back and increasing overall customer satisfaction by at least 10 percent.

When studying what their key competitor was doing differently, top managers could identify only one tangible difference—a shop floor logistical control system the competitor had invested in two years earlier. As a result, they concluded this was the source of their competitor's strength. Before proceeding with a similar investment, however, they wanted to confirm that their instincts were correct and that they could expect to achieve the 10 percent improvement they sought. If not, they wanted to devise a strategy that would enable them to do so. They used our outcome-driven methodology to help them achieve this objective. There were four major steps:

1. Defining and targeting opportunities
2. Evaluating the shop floor logistical control system
3. Quantifying the value of different concepts
4. Generating a breakthrough concept

Step 1: Defining and Targeting Opportunities

P&W used the methods described in Chapter 2 to uncover the customer's desired outcomes. They captured eighty-five outcomes in total—outcomes that customers use to measure how well a vendor executes the job of producing machined parts for new jet engine designs. Once those eighty-five outcomes were known, P&W's manufacturing and services division created and administered a quantitative survey to a portion of its existing and potential customer base to capture the importance of each desired outcome and the degree to which each outcome was currently satisfied by P&W and its key competitor. Then, P&W used the opportunity algorithm to prioritize the outcomes. For illustrative purposes, Table 8.2 shows ten of the desired outcomes and their corresponding importance, satisfaction, and opportunity values. Using the data, the team was able to determine where the market was underserved and overserved and decided to target for improvement all those outcomes that had opportunity scores of 10.0 and higher. (The opportunities listed in Table 8.2 are not all actual targeted outcomes; some have been changed for purposes of confidentiality.)

Table 8.2 P&W Opportunity Scores

Desired Outcomes	Importance	Satisfaction	Opportunity
Minimize the time it takes to obtain status on an order	8.8	4.4	13.2
Minimize the time it takes to change part tolerances	8.9	5.4	12.3
Minimize the impact that a design change has on the schedule for delivery	9.0	6.0	11.9
Minimize turnaround time on priority orders	6.3	2.5	10.1
Minimize cost overruns	7.2	5.8	8.5
Minimize the time it takes to document design changes	6.6	4.9	8.2
Minimize recurring tooling costs	6.3	6.5	6.3
Minimize the time it takes to deliver a completed part	4.3	3.3	5.3
Minimize the cost of rework	4.4	5.2	4.4
Minimize idle manufacturing time	2.1	2.5	2.1

Upon reviewing the data the team made some initial observations that led them to suspect that the shop floor logistical control system might not be the source of their competitor's strength after all. Few outcomes could be impacted by a shop floor logistical control system, and the one that could, minimizing idle manufacturing time, was shown to be unimportant (2.1 importance score). More analysis was needed to confirm this suspicion. Knowing how customers measured value, the P&W team was ready to test how well the shop floor control system would deliver that value and to devise other solutions that would address the remaining opportunities.

Step 2: Evaluating the Shop Floor Logistical Control System

P&W used an outcome-based customer scorecard, as illustrated in Table 8.3, to make three separate evaluations. They began by quantifying the amount of value that was being delivered by their existing offering and their key competitor's offering. Doing so provided them with a benchmark against which to measure just how much more value the proposed logistical control system would deliver.

To make these first two evaluations, P&W managers used the satisfaction data points captured directly from customers in the quantitative survey. In that survey, customers were asked how satisfied they were with their supplier's ability to achieve each outcome and were asked if their supplier was P&W or its competitor.

Next, the team evaluated the logistical control system to determine how it would help them create additional customer value. To make this evaluation, they went through the list of prioritized outcomes and determined the degree to which the control system would enable them to satisfy each. They concluded that the control system would significantly improve their ability to minimize idle manufacturing time, just as it did for their competitor, improving the satisfaction level from 2.5 to 8.5. This, however, was the only significant improvement that they could see the logistical control system making, and P&W managers noted that, as Table 8.2

showed, minimizing idle manufacturing time was a relatively unimportant outcome and already overserved. Their suspicions regarding the logistical control system strengthened. It did not look like it was the source of their competitor's strength after all. They continued their analysis and quantified the total amount of value delivered by their own current systems and those of their key competitor and compared those figures with the value that would be delivered if they added the control system to the P&W manufacturing floor.

Step 3: Quantifying the Value of Different Concepts

To calculate the amount of value delivered by an existing product or service or a proposed idea, we must do a little math. The calculation we use takes two factors into consideration: the opportunity score of the desired outcome and the level of satisfaction generated by the solution being evaluated. To determine the overall value of the solutions, the P&W team multiplied the weighted opportunity score for each desired outcome by the evaluation rating defined for each solution and then summed up the results for each solution. If a solution were to satisfy all the customer outcomes to the greatest possible degree, it would deliver 100 percent of the value desired by the targeted customers and have a concept score of 100.

Using this evaluation method, P&W determined that the shop floor logistical control system would deliver 49.8 percent of the desired value, while P&W's existing service offering delivered 48.3 percent of the desired value. In other words, the proposed system represented only a 3 percent improvement over their existing offering, not the 10 percent improvement the team was anticipating. As the team had observed earlier, the control system did little to address the greatest opportunities for improvement, such as obtaining quick status on an order, and therefore failed to create significant customer value.

Using the same calculation, P&W uncovered some other disturbing news. They learned that their competitor's offering was delivering 11 percent more value than P&W's own (53.4 percent versus 48.3 percent), shedding some light on recent declines in market share. Table 8.3 revealed that P&W's key competitor was significantly better at minimizing turnaround time on priority orders (4.5 versus 2.5) and minimizing the time it took to obtain status on an order (5.1 versus 4.4). The P&W management team finally concluded that it was the systems the competitor had in place to address these other outcomes that were the true source of the competitor's strength, not the logistical control system.

Unwilling to invest in a solution that would deliver only incremental value and intent on leapfrogging their competitor, the team members wisely decided to abandon the plan to invest in the shop floor logistical control system. The vice president who suggested

Table 8.3 P&W Customer Scorecard for Concept Evaluations

Desired Outcomes	P&W Service	Competitor's Service	Logistical Control System	Breakthrough Solution
Minimize the time it takes to obtain status on an order	4.4	5.1	4.4	7.5
Minimize the time it takes to change part tolerances	5.4	6.0	5.4	7.0
Minimize the impact a design change has on the delivery schedule	6.0	5.5	6.0	7.5
Minimize turnaround time on priority orders	2.5	4.5	2.5	6.0
Minimize cost overruns	5.8	5.1	5.8	6.5
Minimize the time it takes to document design changes	4.9	4.6	4.9	6.0
Minimize recurring tooling costs	6.5	7.1	6.5	8.0
Minimize the time it takes to deliver a completed part	3.3	4.2	3.3	4.5
Minimize the cost of rework	5.2	4.7	5.2	6.5
Minimize idle manufacturing time	2.5	8.5	8.5	3.2
	48.3	**53.4**	**49.8**	**66.7**

they look at the control system to begin with was the first to concede that the proposed solution would have failed and was grateful that its problems were identified early on, at the conceptual stage, rather than months down the road after resources had been committed. Everyone realized that they needed a more innovative solution if they were to make gainful improvements in customer satisfaction and achieve their growth objectives.

Step 4: Generating a Breakthrough Concept

P&W team members realized that little stood in the way of their creating a solution that would satisfy their customers' underserved outcomes. Keeping in mind that P&W's existing offering generated only 48.3 percent of all the value that was desired, team members embarked upon a two-day ideation session with the objective of devising a solution that would deliver at least 25 percent more value than their existing offering. A 25 percent improvement would require a solution that delivered 60.4 percent of all the desired value. The multidisciplinary team began by focusing (in priority order) on the opportunities for improvement defined in Table 8.4.

They first generated several ideas that would enable them to minimize the time it took to obtain status on an order. They documented the ideas as they went along, detailing the specifications so as to make the ideas tangible. With a few good ideas to choose from, they determined which would generate the most value for the least cost, effort, and risk. They agreed that the best solution would be a customer-accessible, network-based tracking system that was updated in real time at each step of the manufacturing process. This would allow the customer to obtain an accurate status report in just minutes, rather than hours. This idea, they concluded, would increase the customer satisfaction level from 4.4 to at least 7.5, increasing the value delivered by their offering from 48.3 percent to 51.8 percent, as shown in Table 8.4.

Table 8.4   Ideas Generated by the P&W Team

Desired Outcomes	Idea/Feature	Added Value
Minimize the time it takes to obtain status on an order	Centralized order status tracking system that is customer accessible and updated in real time	51.8
Minimize the time it takes to change part tolerances	Communication system enabling manufacturing and engineering to confer in real time, so non-conformances are identified and rectified quickly	55.0
Minimize the impact that a design change has on the delivery schedule	Cross-training of workers to allow for improved workflow	57.8
Minimize turnaround time on priority orders	Fixed pricing and pooling of a percentage of profits into an overrun "bucket"	60.3
Minimize cost overruns	Fixed pricing and pooling of a percentage of profits into an overrun "bucket"	62.5
All others	All others	66.7

Next they addressed the customers' desire to minimize the time it took to change part tolerances, again generating a small number of good ideas and selecting the one that would generate the most value for acceptable levels of cost, effort, and risk. They concluded that a real-time communications system, one that automatically notified the customer of nonconformance and provided them with a mechanism to accept or modify the suggested tolerance change, would reduce tolerance change time from forty-eight hours to about two hours. They projected that this would increase customer satisfaction from 5.4 to 7.0 and the value of their offering by another 2.35 percent, to 55.0.

When considering their customers' desire to minimize cost overruns, the P&W team decided it could eliminate this problem altogether by moving away from its cost-plus contracts where possible and offering fixed pricing. To make this feasible, the team decided to create an overrun "bucket" that pooled a small percent of the profits from each project into a fund that would be used to contain cost overruns. This idea, members agreed, would increase customer satisfaction from 5.8 to 6.5 and contribute to the overall improvement of their offering.

This ideation methodology was followed for each of the top opportunities. In the end, the P&W team generated about a dozen new ideas (not hundreds), most of which had never been considered before, and selected those that would produce the greatest increases in customer satisfaction, five of which are shown in Table 8.4.

The solution the team selected for implementation, which incorporated ten unique ideas or features, was projected to improve the value of P&W's offering to 66.7 percent, a dramatic 38 percent improvement over the company's existing offering and a 25 percent improvement over that of their competitor—by all measures a breakthrough solution. The solution included new software tools, communication systems, training programs, and new scheduling and pricing programs, but not the shop floor logistical control system that was initially proposed. As an added benefit, the team determined that this highly valued solution required only half the investment that the control system had been projected to require. With newfound conviction and unanimous management approval, they chose to implement this strategy.

Reflecting on this project, P&W team members commented openly that they never would have thought to pursue this course of action if not for the insight they gained into their customers' desired outcomes. From an organizational perspective this information helped them end internal competition and turf wars by providing a basis for agreement.

Before they could begin implementing the proposed solution, the team had to prepare the financial justification, which was surprisingly easy. Usually P&W managers required a proposed initiative to be able to promise a 20 percent return on investment before they would go ahead with it. In this case, however, the managers felt that the 38 percent increase in customer satisfaction that the solution was anticipated to produce was far better incentive for making the investment because an increase in customer satisfaction is far more predictive of growth and revenue than return on investment is. One year after implementation, the solution had already increased customer satisfaction by 35 percent—closely approaching the amount of value the model had predicted it would deliver.

In less than two years, P&W regained their lost market share and also captured an additional five percentage points because they implemented a solution they knew would satisfy their customers' desired outcomes, thereby delivering value and generating growth. With this success behind it, P&W used the same methodology to improve their advanced composite-material testing services. Here they reduced the cost of testing a composite material from $4 million to $435,000 and reduced development cycle time by 75 percent, from two years to six months.

What Is the Role of R&D in the Innovation Process?

We have discussed how a company creates value by targeting a set of opportunities (underserved outcomes) and exploiting them for revenue gains in three distinct ways: by selling more of their currently available products and services by better communicating any advantages these offerings have in satisfying the targeted underserved outcomes; by quickly bringing to market those products and services in the development pipeline that do the best job of addressing the targeted opportunities; and by developing product and service ideas that hit the remaining unexploited opportunities through the systematic creation of new and potentially breakthrough concepts. One other possibility for value creation, however, must be considered.

If a company is unable to address one or more targeted outcomes with their current products, with the products the company has in the pipeline, or with focused brainstorming efforts, then outcome-driven companies will typically send those remaining underserved outcomes to R&D as targets for technology development or to the management and acquisition team as targets for acquisition. Motorola treated those hard-to-address outcomes as targets for technology development when they asked their long-term mobile radio technology development team to work on a number of outcomes related to superior voice command technology. The advantage of handing hard-to-address outcomes to R&D is that it guarantees a company that R&D efforts are focused on solving an important customer problem, with the eventual result being value creation. Not many organizations can say with confidence that their R&D efforts, if successful, will produce a product, service, or product feature that customers will want. But with insight into the opportunities that exist in a market, a company can prioritize R&D efforts and focus resources on efforts that are likely to pay off. At the same time they can abort efforts that address outcomes that are unimportant or overserved. The end result is more successful R&D efforts in less time and at less cost. Adding this efficiency is bound to improve an organization's bottom line and give the R&D team an operational competitive advantage.

Finally, a company can address certain underserved outcomes through solid acquisition strategies. Companies often shop around to see what other companies have the technologies they need to effectively address the outcomes that are underserved in their markets.

Summary

There is no guarantee that a company's existing products and those in the pipeline will address all or even any of the opportunities they have identified and targeted, especially if the company is new to the market. To address the remaining opportunities, a company must either think of new, potentially breakthrough products or product features that will satisfy the remaining underserved outcomes, or the company must acquire technology (through licensing or acquisition) that enables the company to satisfy the targeted outcomes.

Most brainstorming and idea-generation efforts yield inadequate results because managers don't focus their employees' creativity, solicit too many ideas, and cannot judge the value of employees' efforts. Companies do not need to generate hundreds of ideas; they need to generate just a handful of ideas that specifically and satisfactorily address their customers' underserved outcomes. Therefore, companies should focus their energies on generating ideas around the underserved outcomes. This will increase the likelihood that the time spent will result in ideas that are worthy of pursuit. We have five guidelines for ideation sessions:

- Stay focused on the targets
- Aim for breakthrough improvement
- Constrain thinking to enhance creativity
- Eliminate bad ideas quickly
- Optimize the best idea for cost, effort, risk, and sustainability

After the ideation sessions have been completed, companies are faced with the daunting task of evaluating the ideas that have been generated. Companies that follow our outcome-driven methods avoid the common pitfalls of the evaluation process because objective company team members, and not customers, evaluate ideas for their ability to satisfy all the outcomes customers are trying to achieve when performing a job. Unlike customers, company team members know the impact a technology will have on an outcome and have the discipline to assess an idea against all the outcomes.

When companies get the evaluation process right, they are able to determine which ideas are worthy of pursuit and which are not.

They avoid guesswork, indecision, and disastrous wrong bets and create more breakthrough solutions—and more growth—in less time and with fewer resources. Consider the impact this level of improvement will have on a company's bottom line, on productivity, and on the economy in general. The outcome-driven paradigm provides the foundation upon which to make these improvements, transforming innovation into a quantifiable and predictable discipline.

Epilogue

Tactical Tips for Managers

The outcome-driven approach to innovation is logical, quantitative, practical, and proven, so why isn't it standard practice in industry today? The reason is that it requires companies (executives, managers, and employees) to think differently about innovation, learn new skills, and, most importantly, give up what feels natural. What could be more natural than asking customers how they would like to see a product improved and then acting on the feedback? When a product is under development, it is natural for people to feel enthusiastic about it, even if the enthusiasm is unwarranted and the product will ultimately fail. Similarly, it is natural for companies to pursue ideas that fit within the current business model or align with existing competencies, even though doing so may mean inadvertently overlooking opportunities with greater potential for growth. Lastly, it is easier (and therefore feels more natural) to test a new product or service's value after it has been created than it is to figure out how customers measure value and build a solution in accordance with those measures. But however natural old habits feel, they result in otherwise logical companies making irresponsible decisions. In what other business process is a 50 to 90 percent failure rate acceptable? None. So what has to change?

As the past chapters have suggested, to become outcome driven, a firm must change its approach to market research, idea generation, concept evaluation, and concept design. Companies must have an innovation strategy—a defined, conscious approach to innovation. Managers must focus employee creativity on underserved jobs, outcomes, and constraints and put an end to unfocused, scattershot brainstorming. Companies must take the responsibility of devising new product concepts away from customers and lead users and put it back in the hands of the strategists who know whom to target and the engineers, designers, programmers, materials experts, technologists, and others who have the knowledge and creativity to see beyond what exists today. Becoming outcome driven is not easy—but those companies that have the motivation and discipline to transform their practices are building a competitive advantage through innovation.

Having worked with dozens of companies that have adopted outcome-driven thinking and having observed where the difficulties lie, we have come up with ten tips that may make the process easier. These tactical tips have helped companies overcome some intrinsic barriers to success.

1. *Bring precision to the language of innovation.* To start, executives must change the way managers and employees think and talk about innovation and provide them with a common language for doing so. Rather than talking about how the voice of the customer reveals customers' wants and needs, managers and employees must talk about helping customers get functional and emotional jobs done and satisfying their underserved desired outcomes. Managers and employees must know the difference between solutions, specifications, needs, benefits, and outcomes. They must talk about broad market opportunities and segments of opportunity. Executives must reinforce the idea throughout the firm that customers indeed use a set of metrics to measure how effectively they are able to get a job done and that the company can use those same metrics to guide the creation of products. Managers and

employees must talk about product, operational, and disruptive innovation and know how these types of innovation differ from one another. The terms we use throughout this book are precise. We offer them as a common language in which innovation can be discussed, understood, and evolved. (See the glossary for more details and for specific definitions.)

2. *Separate the roles and the information-related needs of marketing and development.* Unclear demarcation between the roles and assignments of marketing and development often plague the innovation process. Although the basic objective of marketing is to market and sell the company's products and the basic role of development is to create new products and services, somehow over the years the marketing function has inherited the responsibility of providing the development function with customer information so development can create new products—but the results have been problematic.

As we have seen, in most firms marketing gathers information on how and when customers make purchases and on how to reach customers. Marketing personnel uncover customer needs so they can fine-tune their sales pitch, and they ask customers what features they want to see in future products. They then proudly pass this information on to development, but as we have learned, developers cannot use this type of information to make product and design decisions. Development requires far more detailed information than marketing typically provides, so in the end both parties are frustrated and development is shortchanged.

So what is the solution? Companies must clearly separate the responsibilities and information needs of marketing and development. Marketing should continue to gather customer information for marketing, sales, and advertising purposes and should segment for these purposes as well; but companies should not force this information on development and expect it to make gold out of hay. If marketing wants to provide development with data that is useful for developers, then it must learn what information is needed (jobs, outcomes, constraints, and segments of opportunity) and acquire the skills to obtain that information—otherwise development should be empowered to gather the information on its own. Turf battles have often been fought between marketing and development over which function should obtain the customer inputs necessary for development, but it is time for those battles to end. Responsibility—and budget—should go to whichever function shoulders the responsibility.

3. *Expand the role of research and the market researcher.* Most companies find it difficult to justify proactive market research of the sort we recommend in this book, although they think nothing of spending money on validating ideas through focus groups and conjoint analysis and on measuring past performance through customer satisfaction studies. Research that could help define a product or service concept is often shortcut or skipped because getting a product out the door quickly often takes precedence over getting the right product out the door. Companies may not have the time to do it right, but they have the time to do it over. This thinking must stop. Regardless of where market researchers reside (in marketing or development, on product teams, or as a centralized function), companies must understand that getting the right customer data is critical to success and must ensure that the needed funding is available. It may be difficult to quantify the Return on Investment (ROI) in the traditional sense, but if a company wants to ensure its resources are focused on winning products it is unreasonable to expect that it can be done without basic knowledge of the customers' outcomes.

In addition, companies must stop thinking that market researchers can only be reactive data collectors; instead, they must push their researchers to become proactive strategists who uncover areas of opportunity in a market, inform marketing and development of those opportunities, and work with those functions to ensure that the opportunities are addressed. Companies such as Microsoft conduct job-based research without being asked to do so by any development or marketing team. The researchers inform the relevant constituents of the opportunities that are uncovered and direct them to use that information to create new markets and customer value. Expanding the role of the market researcher in this manner may make companies (and even some researchers) uncomfortable, but having researchers who understand the concept of outcome-based innovation and know how to obtain, prioritize, and apply the needed information is critical to improving innovation.

4. *Treat the adoption of outcome-driven innovation as an investment in infrastructure.* Many companies have spent considerable time and effort implementing Customer Relationship Management (CRM) systems to improve the marketing and sales process and Enterprise Resource Planning (ERP) infrastructure to improve resource management. Adoption of outcome-driven innovation should be thought of the same way—as an investment in infrastructure made to improve a critical business process and give the company a competitive advantage. This investment pays for itself through the creation of many valued products and reduction in wasted development expense. Successfully reinventing the innovation process means more valued products in less time and at less cost.

5. *Use existing internal networks to initiate outcome-driven innovation.* Many manufacturing companies have adopted the Design for Six Sigma philosophy and have teams of individuals trained in six sigma philosophies and principles, for example, black belts, green belts, etc., organized throughout their firms. Service organizations that have adopted the Baldridge National Quality Program standards (the service equivalent to Six Sigma) have similar programs and struc-

tures. Initiating outcome-driven innovation through these networks increases the chance of success by drawing on pre-existing dedicated teams that can be trained to conduct research and facilitate idea-generation sessions in different parts of the organization. Although most of the organization should be familiar with the thinking behind outcome-driven innovation, only a handful of company employees need to be skilled at conducting the required research and working with teams to use the data. Training black belts and others to capture customer outcomes and conduct outcome-based market research—or making researchers black belts—can speed up the impact of outcome-driven thinking in a company that is already organized in this manner.

6. *Abandon the ineffective and time-consuming approaches of the past.* In conjunction with introducing outcome-driven innovation, companies should abandon the failed approaches of the past—approaches such as Quality Function Deployment (QFD), which has had only limited success in demystifying the fuzzy front end of the product development process. Don't get us wrong, QFD does have some benefits, but trying to turn a tool (such as the Matrix-based House of Quality) that was intended to improve manufacturing reliability into a tool for new product innovation is like trying to build a skyscraper on the foundation of a single-family home. From our experience, people implementing the QFD process become more intent on ensuring that the time-consuming matrix associated with the House of Quality is filled out than on defining solid principles for innovation. Innovation does not have to revolve around filling out a matrix. The only reason matrix analysis is needed at all is to compensate for the fact that undisciplined methods are used to collect customer inputs. If from the start companies use the metrics that customers use to measure value (desired outcomes), there is no need for a matrix, and the time and money companies have

hitherto spent filling it out can be fruitfully refocused on other activities.

In addition, companies should continue to use ideas and tools that have been helpful—but they should not misapply them. Lead users, for example, are a great source of ideas, but by definition they represent only a small percentage of the user population. The ideas lead users come up with should be evaluated against the underserved outcomes of the target population. What is good for lead users may not be saleable to the rest of the user population.

7. *Share needed information across the organization.* Innovation data is one of the most important assets a company can own. Yet, it is often found in an uncategorized pile of reports on a research manager's desk or in a file cabinet in some corporate building. Rarely does research have a shelf life longer than six months, but because of the stable nature of outcomes and jobs, the innovation data collected here has a shelf life measured in years. The key is to get that information into the hands, and on the desktops, of those who can benefit from it the most.

Only when all key employees know where the opportunities exist in a market will a company be able to focus the creativity of the entire organization on value creation. In some firms customer information can be disseminated through the organization via an internal Web portal. In addition, at Strategyn we typically offer companies access to the report generation system we use internally to analyze project data. These handy reports make it much easier to share information across the organization in a format that is suitable for decision making. Sharing customer information across the organization not only optimizes the use of the collected data to accelerate the creation of customer value, but as a side benefit, it also helps to ensure that research efforts are not being duplicated in different parts of the company.

8. *Get started with internal projects—embrace operational innova-tion.* For those companies and individuals who want to apply outcome-driven thinking on their own (that is without third party training or assistance) we suggest that they start with internal company innovation—that is, process innovation applied to internal services, human resources (HR), manu-facturing, and so on. This way, companies can hone their innovation skills and make improvements with little risk of public failure. In addition, internal projects cost far less to execute because the cost of qualitative and quantitative research is eliminated. Interviewing company employees to uncover their outcomes and prioritizing those outcomes with an internally created and administered questionnaire requires only time—no research budget. Once a company has one or two successes under their belt, they will be more confident about applying the same thinking to product innovation and have the skill set to obtain the needed information from external customers.

9. *Repurpose the customer satisfaction study.* Customer satisfaction studies represent one of the largest research expenditures in many organizations. They involve extensive sample sizes and are used to drive initiatives to improve customer retention. However, these studies are often wrought with vague terms (solutions, specifications, needs, and benefits) that make it dif-ficult to assess how to add or create customer value.

In some cases it makes good sense to include questions relating to customer outcomes along with the traditional cus-tomer satisfaction questions so that the study can be used both to gauge customer satisfaction and for purposes of development. By adding outcome-focused questions, the study becomes a helpful research tool, and the questions can be added without affecting the budget. As we discussed in Chapter 3, companies gain a more detailed view of the com-petition by comparing how all competitors satisfy the collec-tive set of customer outcomes. This tip will only work well for companies that routinely conduct customer satisfaction studies in each of their markets. If the company performs one big study across all the markets in which they are active, the results will not be useful, because the outcomes for many different customer jobs will be mixed together, making such a study impractical.

10. *Treat the discovered opportunities as sacred.* Too many times we see companies conduct outcome-based research and discover a number of great opportunities, only to then fail to treat them as opportunities. Some companies apparently don't want to believe what they have discovered. Others struggle to accept that it is possible to have all the opportunities laid out right in front of them—just like that. Others yet feel that, like all other studies in the past, this information is the "flavor of the month," and if they ignore it long enough it will go away and they can continue to do what they want. If this works, then they will not have to face the hard decision of cutting efforts on projects that people are working on in favor of other new projects. In each of these situations, companies just don't realize the ramifications of what they have discovered. Having every opportunity in a market listed in priority order is invaluable and should be treated as such.

These opportunities should be embraced, not questioned. They should be communicated to relevant company employees and acted upon. Once a company knows where the opportunities lie in a market, they should reward employees for finding ways to satisfy those underserved outcomes. These opportunities are real, and customers are waiting for them to be addressed. They should become the focal point for innovation.

The ideas put forth in this book have produced highly valued, even breakthrough, products and services for many companies throughout the world. They are logical, practical, and proven. That is not to say they cannot be improved—they can be. We are committed to making improvements to the process every time we employ it and have been since we started. We ask that you commit to do the same. As you employ outcome-driven thinking please feel free to share your thoughts, successes, and failures with us at ideas@strategyn.com. Together we can evolve the innovation process, forever changing the way value is created for customers and profit is generated for companies.

Glossary

Benefit: A statement that describes the tangible advantage that a customer would like a new product or service to deliver. Benefit statements include words or phrases such as "easy to use," "convenient," "faster," "better," and "cheaper." Although benefit statements are commonly offered up by customers when they are asked for their requirements, they are not useful inputs when it comes to creating valued new products and services.

Breakthrough concept: A concept that will deliver customers significant new value. Most successful new products will improve the satisfaction ratings of underserved outcomes between 5 and 10 percent, while breakthrough products typically improve the satisfaction level by 20 percent or more.

Broad-market opportunities: Underserved outcomes that are common to all segments of the customer population, or underserved jobs or constraints that are found in all segments of the population.

Cluster analysis: An analysis technique that finds groups of customers who value the same underserved desired outcomes. This technique is used in the outcome-driven innovation process to segment markets and discover segments of opportunity.

Concept: An idea or potential solution in its theoretical stage.

Concept evaluation and testing: A method used to evaluate a concept's potential for delivering value to customers in a specified target segment.

Constraint: A roadblock that prevents customers from getting a job done altogether or under a certain circumstance. Constraints are often physical, regulatory, or environmental in nature. Not being able to make a cell phone call from inside a building is a constraint to use. Constraints often represent excellent growth opportunities and make good targets for innovation.

Consumer: The end user of a product or service. A subset of all customers (customers being a larger group comprising distributors, purchasers, influencers, end users, etc.). Also defined as someone who already uses a product or service.

Customer: Any person or entity in the value chain that could be targeted for value creation (for example, distributor, purchaser, influencer, and end user). In the medical industry customers may include surgeons, support staff, hospital administrators, regulators, and buyers.

Customer driven: An orientation that dictates that companies understand what their customers want before they invest in the creation of a new product or service. This commonsense approach to innovation started in the mid-1980s but has only had modest success making the innovation process more efficient.

Customer scorecard: A quantitative method used to evaluate the degree to which a new product concept satisfies customers' underserved (and overserved) outcomes. Using this tool, a concept's value can be measured in advance of its actual development—at the conceptual stage.

Customer value model: The collective set of outcomes that define how customers are trying to get a job done. The value model is often represented in a process-flow diagram with outcomes defined for each step of the job.

Design for Six Sigma: A measure of quality that strives for near perfection. Six Sigma is a disciplined, data-driven approach and methodology for eliminating defects. The goal is six standard deviations between the mean and the nearest specification limit, or no more than 3.4 defects per million. This standard can be applied to any process—including innovation.

Desired competitive position: A unique and valued competitive position that is achieved when a product satisfies the most underserved desired outcomes better than any solution employed or planned by a competitor.

Development pipeline: The set of product and service initiatives that companies have underway but have not yet launched. In the outcome-driven environment, initiatives in the pipeline are prioritized to determine which ones will do the best job of satisfying the customers' underserved outcomes.

Emotional jobs: Tasks that relate to achieving personal goals. Emotional jobs are subdivided into personal jobs (how people want to feel in a given circumstance) and social jobs (how people want to be perceived by others). A personal job associated with an automobile, for example, may be to feel young, and a social job associated with an automobile may be to be perceived as successful by others.

External customer: Customers that are outside the organization. Examples include other equipment manufacturers (OEMs), distributors, purchasers, and end users. External customers are typically part of the value chain.

Factor analysis: A technique that identifies a number of dimensions (factors) that explain the majority of the interrelationships (correlations) among variables. In the case of outcome-driven innovation, the variables are outcomes. If two outcomes are consistently rated in a parallel manner, then they will be placed in the same factor. This technique is used in the outcome-driven segmentation process to identify the segmentation variables.

Focused brainstorming: The process of generating a handful of valuable ideas by focusing creativity on customers' underserved outcomes. This is in contrast to traditional brainstorming, which uses a scattershot approach to generate hundreds of ideas of questionable value.

Functional jobs: Nonemotional tasks that people seek to accomplish. An automobile, for example, helps people with the functional job of moving passengers and belongings from one location to another. (Compare this with the emotional jobs associated with an automobile, described above.) The outcomes associated with functional jobs are typically the focal point for value creation, while the outcomes associated with emotional jobs often provide ideas for effective positioning and marketing.

Ideation (idea generation): The process of creating new ideas that are focused on addressing a set of targeted underserved outcomes, jobs, and constraints.

Importance and satisfaction data: Data on the importance and satisfaction that people place on a specified set of desired outcomes, jobs, or constraints. In outcome-driven innovation, these data are quantifiable and are obtained through statistically valid research.

Importance rating: A numerical value a customer gives an outcome, job, or constraint, reflecting how greatly the customer desires to achieve the outcome, perform the job, or overcome the constraint.

Innovation: The process of creating a product or service solution that delivers significant new customer value. The process begins with the selection of the customer and market, includes the identification and prioritization of opportunities, and ends with the creation of an innovative product or service.

Internal customer: Customers that are within an organization. Examples include employees, managers, and executives.

Job: A task or activity that individuals or businesses are trying to get done. To get the job done, they seek out helpful products and services. For example, individuals buy insurance policies to reduce financial risk, and businesses buy CRM tools to help them manage customer leads and sales activities. Job statements are a key input in the innovation process because once companies know what jobs customers are trying to get done, they can create products and services that will help customers with those jobs.

Job-based segmentation: Segmentation that uses job statements (and their opportunity scores), rather than outcomes, as its basis. Cluster analysis is executed to create the segments. The segments are then profiled to determine their composition. The result is the creation of segments of opportunity, which can be used to find altogether new markets. Outcome-based segmentation, by comparison, identifies opportunities within a market.

Kurtosis: A measure of the extent to which observations cluster around a central point. For a normal distribution, the value of the kurtosis statistic is 0. Positive kurtosis indicates that the observations cluster more than those in the normal distribution, and negative kurtosis indicates the observations cluster less. The kurtosis value helps determine which outcomes should be used as the bases for outcome-driven segmentation.

Lateral thinking: A form of thinking used for problem solving that involves looking at the problem from unusual or unexpected angles.

Low-end disruption: Targeting a low-cost technology at a segment of core-market customers who are overserved with the current products and services and are willing to accept a less costly, lower-performance product. This strategy disrupts the existing business model and provides a beachhead from which to eventually attract mainstream customers.

Need: A statement made by customers that is expressed as an abstract description of the overall quality of a product or service. Needs are typically stated as adjectives and do not imply a specific benefit to the customer. Customers commonly say, for example, that they require a product or service to be "reliable," "effective," "strong," "powerful," "robust," and so on. Although these statements are commonly offered up by customers when they are asked for their requirements, they are not useful inputs when it comes to creating valued new products and services.

Needs-based segmentation: Segmentation that uses customers' needs as its basis. This approach is not recommended because little discipline typically goes into defining just what "needs" are, and many different types of inputs (solutions, specifications, needs, benefits, outcomes) are typically incorporated into the analysis. This results in inaccurate and often misleading segmentation schemes.

New-market disruption: Targeting a new set of customers (nonconsumers) who do not have the skill or wealth needed to acquire and use available products.

New-market innovation: Innovation that is made possible when a company discovers that individuals or businesses are struggling to get a job done and devises a creative product or service that enables those individuals or businesses to do the job faster and cheaper than hitherto possible. Ultimately, the company creates a new market.

Nonconsumer: Individuals or businesses that lack the skill or wealth needed to acquire and use available products.

Operational innovation: Innovation in how a company runs. Operational innovation involves improving internal business processes, such as distribution, sales, manufacturing, and human resource management. This type of innovation often requires companies to take apart their value chains and reconstruct them in ways that cut costs and waste.

Opportunity: An outcome, job, or constraint that is underserved and attractive for improvement or overserved and a good target for cost reduction. Opportunities are prioritized using the opportunity algorithm.

Opportunity algorithm: A formula for determining the degree to which a job, outcome, or constraint is underserved or overserved. The formula states that opportunity equals importance plus the difference between importance and satisfaction, where that difference is not allowed to go below zero: opportunity = [importance + max (importance − satisfaction, 0)].

The value for importance for each attribute (job, outcome, or constraint) equals the percentage of people rating that attribute a 4 or a 5 on a scale of 1 to 5, where 1 = not important, and 5 = very important. The percentages are placed on a 10-point scale, so an attribute that 75 percent of the population rated a 4 or a 5 for importance would be put into the algorithm as 7.5. The value for satisfaction for each attribute is calculated and put into the algorithm in the same manner.

Outcome: A metric that customers use to measure how well they are getting a job done. Outcomes are customers' fundamental measures of product or service performance, and they are inherent to the execution of a specific job and a key input in the innovation process. Customers have these metrics in their minds, but they seldom articulate them, and companies rarely understand them. Organizations do not generally collect this information because they do not recognize its central role in the creation of breakthrough products and services.

Outcome-based brand: A brand that describes the job that customers are tying to get done. For example, the toolmaker Milwaukee calls its reciprocating saw the Sawzall, a name that describes the job the tool is designed to perform—cutting through anything. Outcome-based brands connect with customers because they tie a product to a job.

Outcome-based messaging: A marketing communication that ties a product feature to an outcome.

Outcome-based segmentation: Segmentation that uses outcomes (and their opportunity scores) as its basis. Cluster analysis is executed to create the segments. The segments are then profiled to determine their composition. This results in the creation of segments of opportunity. Outcome-based segmentation is used to find opportunities within a market, whereas job-based segmentation is used to find altogether new markets.

Outcome driven: An innovation philosophy in which companies uncover customers' measures of value (outcomes), determine which are underserved, and work systematically to devise new solutions that address the opportunities and deliver significant new customer value.

Overserved: The condition that is present when jobs, outcomes, or constraints that are unimportant to the customer are very satisfied by the products and services available today. The degree to which jobs, outcomes, or constraints are overserved is quantified by using the opportunity algorithm. Overserved jobs, outcomes, or constraints are often targets for cost reduction.

Product innovation: Innovation from improvements that are made to products. With service innovation, it is the most common form of innovation.

Qualitative research: In the context of outcome-driven innovation, research that is used to uncover the key inputs into innovation—jobs, outcomes, and constraints. Group interviews, personal interviews, and observational research are all methods used to obtain this information.

Quantitative research: In the context of outcome-driven innovation, research that is conducted to quantify the importance and satisfaction level of the key customer inputs—jobs, outcomes, and constraints. Web and phone-based surveys are commonly used to conduct this research.

Requirement: Generally speaking, any expression of what customers expect from a product—wants, needs, benefits, solutions, ideas, desires, demands, specifications, and so on. The term's vagueness has contributed to the ineffectiveness of the customer-driven movement.

Satisfaction rating: A numerical expression of how satisfied an individual is that an outcome is well served, a job is able to be done well, or a constraint minimally interferes with jobs or outcomes.

Segment: A group of customers that is homogeneous in its desire to achieve a certain set of outcomes or to get certain jobs done.

Segmentation: The grouping of customers into meaningful categories, in this case for the purpose of value creation and innovation.

Segment-specific opportunities: Outcomes that are underserved in specific outcome-based segments, or jobs that are underserved in specific job-based segments.

Service innovation: Innovation from improvements that are made to services. With product innovation, it is the most common form of innovation.

Solution: A statement made by customers that describes the physical or tangible features they want to see in a product or service they use. For instance, customers may tell a razor manufacturer that they want a rubberized handle or a lubrication strip on the razor head. Although these statements are commonly offered up by customers when they are asked for their requirements, they are not useful inputs when it comes to creating valued new products and services.

Specification: A statement made by customers that gives a company detailed instructions on particular design characteristics—size, weight, color, and shape. Razor users may request a wider handle or a lighter weight. Although these statements are commonly offered up by customers when they are asked for their requirements, they are not useful inputs when it comes to creating valued new products and services.

Stakeholder: An individual or group in a company who has an interest in or is responsible for the creation of a product, service, or strategy.

Statistical process control (SPC): A tool used by manufacturers to control manufacturing process variability and ensure a predictable result.

Targeting (opportunities): The art of selecting a set of underserved outcomes and jobs that an organization will target for improvement and value creation.

Technology driven: An innovation philosophy in which companies first create a new technology and then attempt to find markets for it. This is an inefficient approach to innovation.

Theme: A category under which one can group related underserved outcomes. For example, a number of outcomes on wound-care products might be grouped under "preventing complications"— even though none of the outcomes may directly mention preventing complications. Discovering a theme is useful for positioning, messaging, and branding purposes.

Underserved: The condition that is present when jobs, outcomes, or constraints that are important to the customer are unsatisfied by the products and services available today. The degree to which jobs, outcomes, or constraints are underserved is quantified by using the opportunity algorithm.

Value chain: The collective set of customers that a company must contend with to ensure the success of its products and services. The value chain may include OEMs, distributors, purchasers, end users, or other customers.

Value migration: The movement of opportunities in the value chain and for specific customers over time. Value migrates as formerly underserved outcomes are addressed and therefore cease to be underserved. New value can then be generated only by finding other underserved outcomes.

Variance: A measure of dispersion around the mean, equal to the sum of the squared deviations from the mean divided by one less than the number of cases. The variance is measured in units that are the square of the variable itself.

Voice of the customer: The idea of listening to customers for the purpose of understanding their requirements. This approach has had limited success because the literal voice of the customer typically provides information in the form of solutions, specifications, needs, and benefits—not in the form of outcomes, jobs, and constraints, which is the form that is necessary for successful innovation.

Bibliography

Christensen, Clayton M., and Michael E. Raynor. *The Innovator's Solution: Creating and Sustaining Successful Growth*. Boston, MA: Harvard Business School Press, 2003.

Hesseldahl, Arik. "The Return of Iridium." Forbes.com.

Porter, Michael. "What Is Strategy?" *Harvard Business Review*, November–December 1996.

Schindler, Robert M. "The Real Lesson of New Coke: The Value of Focus Groups for Predicting the Effects of Social Influence." *Marketing Research*, December 1992.

Slywotsky, Adrian J. *Value Migration*. Boston, MA: Harvard Business School Press, 1983.

Ulwick, Anthony W. "Turn Customer Input into Innovation." *Harvard Business Review*, January 2002.

Yankelovich, Daniel. "New Criteria for Market Segmentation." *Harvard Business Review*, March–April 1964.

Index

Customer-driven approach,
to innovation, xiv
analyzing, xvi
Customer-driven inputs, vs.
outcome-driven puts,
for innovation, 37–39
Customer-jobs matrix, 6–9
Customers
determining decision-
making criteria of, xvi
outcome-based market
segmentation for
identifying
demanding, 76
outcome-based market
segmentation for
identifying
unattractive, 76–77
types of data companies
collect from, 19–22
visits, xiv

Data
customer-driven, vs.
outcome-driven, for
innovation, 37–39
from customers, 19–22
knowing which type of, to
collect, 35–36
methods for obtaining
necessary, 32–34
sharing, across
organizations, 173

for successful innovation,
23–32
constraints, 32
desired outcomes,
26–31
jobs to be done,
23–26
Day-trading markets, 79
Dell, xxiv, 4
Desired outcomes, of
customers, 26–31. *See
also* Outcomes
collecting, at AIG, 33–34
dissection of, 28–29
interviewing for, 28
at Rohm and Hass
Company, 29–30
stability of, 30–31
Development. *See* Research
and development (R&D)
Development, technology,
opportunities for, 89–90
Development departments,
separating roles and
information needs from
marketing departments
and, 169–70
DeWalt, 7, 53–54, 55, 56–57
Disruptive innovation, 4–5.
See also Innovation
using outcome-based
market segmentation
for, 77–78

emotional vs. functional
dimensions of,
108–14
failure of, for promoting
true value of
products, 101–3
outdated, 102–3
prerequisites for effective
strategies for, 103–7
Metrics, that drive
innovation, 26–31
Microsoft Corporation, xxxiv,
80
Motorola, xiii
emotional vs. functional
marketing at, 109–11
identifying market
opportunities at,
74–75
innovation at, 7
marketing strategies at,
113
outcome-based
segmentation for,
69–73
platform development at,
91

Needs, 21
Needs-based segmentation,
xiv, 64. *See also* Market
segmentation
New Coke, xiv

New market innovation, 3
New products, opportunities
for, 87–89
Nike, 114
Nokia, 7, 109
Nortel Networks, 65

Observational research, 33
Operational innovation, 3–4
Opportunities
common mistakes in
prioritizing, 41–44
defined, 40–41
embracing, 175
exploiting, for revenue
gains, 99–100
identifying, xxvi–xxvii
for long-term growth,
89–90
for new, ancillary products,
87–88
prioritizing, 44–48
reasons companies fail to
target key, 95–97
targeting, for growth,
xxviii–xxvi
for technology
development, 89–90
that form themes, 85–87
that represent growth
avenues, 87
types of broad-market,
85–90